MW01700591

MARK PATRICK

WAKE UP SKINNY

The Simple Solution for a Lean and Healthy Body

"IN "WAKE UP SKINNY" YOU'LL DISCOVER THE SHOCKING TRUTH OF HOW OBESITY IS BEING PROMOTED TO MILLIONS. LEARN THE SECRETS THAT COMPANIES PUSHING POPULAR DIETS DON'T WANT YOU TO KNOW. DISCOVER HOW YOUR CURRENT PSYCHOLOGY MIGHT BE MAKING YOUR BODY NEED JUNK FOOD....AND HOW TO TURN IT ALL AROUND STARTING RIGHT NOW."

- MARK PATRICK

DISCLAIMER AND TERMS OF USE AGREEMENT

The author and publisher of this book and the accompanying materials have used the best efforts in preparing this book. The author and publisher make no representation or warranties with respect to the accuracy, applicability, fitness, or completeness of the contents of this book. The information contained in this book is strictly for educational purposes. Therefore, if you wish to apply ideas contained in this book, you are taking full responsibility for your actions and all consequences associated with your actions.

Every effort has been made to accurately represent this book and its potential. Even though this industry is one where we see both rapid and lasting results, there is no guarantee that you will get results using the techniques and ideas in these educational materials. Examples in these materials are not to be interpreted as a personal recommendation, nor are they to be interpreted as representative results. The examples contained in these materials are not typical and, as with any weight loss program, your results may vary. Potential for results is entirely dependent on the person using our products, ideas and techniques, and the manner in which they use the products, ideas and techniques. We do not promote this as a "get thin fast scheme," as, without a well-planned diet and exercise routine, individuals will not achieve results.

Your level of success in attaining the results spoken of in our materials depends on the time you devote to the program, ideas and techniques mentioned, your level of health, and your persistence in taking the appropriate actions on a daily basis. Since these factors differ according to individual, we cannot guarantee your success, your weight loss, or your metabolic enhancement, nor are we responsible for any of your actions.

The author and publisher disclaim any warranties (express or implied), merchantability, or fitness for any particular purpose. The author and publisher shall in no event be held liable to any party for any direct, indirect, punitive, special, mental, physical, incidental, or other consequential damages arising directly or indirectly from any use of this material, which is provided “as is” and without warranties.

The author and publisher of this book recommend that you consult a competent physician before using any of the techniques taught here, and that you use the techniques under their guidance.

The author and publisher do not warrant the performance, effectiveness or application of any sites listed or linked to this book or on our websites. All links are for information purposes only and are not warranted for content, accuracy or any other implied or explicit purpose.

The author and publisher take no responsibility for the contents of and/or representations made on, any sites listed or linked to this book on our websites. Should you have any questions concerning the content of and/or representations made on, those sites, you should directly contact the host of those sites. Any statement made on our company website or in this book that directly relate to dietary supplements has not been evaluated by the food and drug administration.

This book is copyrighted© 2019 Institute of Hypnosis Research, LLC. No part of this publication may be reproduced or utilized in any form or by any means, electronic or mechanical, including photocopying, recording, or by any information storage or retrieval system, without permission in writing from the author.

ACKNOWLEDGEMENTS

It has taken me over 20 years to acquire the knowledge I am about to share with you. As I begin to reflect on the magnitude of this project and the profound impact it has had on so many, I am reminded of those who were instrumental in its development.

First and foremost I wish to thank Joanne my wife for being both a mother and sometimes a father to our children. I thank her for raising two wonderful children and for keeping my life in order while I spent what feels like a lifetime traveling through every nook and cranny of this country meeting some of the most amazing people so that I could learn and apply these skills and bring them to people like you.

Secondly, I would like to thank God for blessing me with two wonderful children Geena and Tina who everyday give me incredible inspiration.

I would also like to thank my parents for their love and my dad for instilling in me an incredible work ethic.

I also have to thank the greatest friends and hardest working speakers in the world Pat, Joe and Frank.

Amongst my greatest sources of inspiration are my clients, who have provided the fuel that keeps me going and who make my passion for life and for living stronger every day. Together we have taken on some incredible undertakings, for this I thank you enthusiastically.

Finally I want to communicate my appreciation to you, the reader, with whom I feel a special bond because you are starting on this journey to a healthier lifestyle. Although you cannot yet see the results in your physical appearance, I know over the next few weeksas you apply the information this book has to offerall of your dreams will come true.

TABLE OF CONTENTS

1

INTRODUCTION

It's Time for a Wake Up Call Let me ask you a question…

What would your life be like if you could literally wake up skinny and healthy, full of energy and life and feeling great about the way you look?

Sounds like a dream, right?

Well, what if your current beliefs about dieting were one hundred percent guaranteed to KEEP you from ever realizing that dream?

Well, guess what….odds are about 95% of the time they will. Concerned?

Keep reading… Imagine this:

An automobile manufacturer puts a car on the market and it becomes a success just about overnight. However, after selling about 10 million units, a major defect arises with the car's performance. In fact, this defect is so severe that it not only debilitates the car and makes it completely impossible to drive; it also puts the driver of the car in mortal danger.

This defect shows up in 95% of the units sold. So what now?

Well, it's a no brainer, isn't it?

Complete recall of all 10 million units and all units on the showroom floor would be a done deal.

Think about it: Even if this manufacturer was an "evil empire" that only cared about the bottom line, do you think they'd spend any time deliberating?

Do you think any reasonable person who owned the car would hesitate to bring it back?

But consider this...

95% of people who lose weight gain it right back.

Now we hear statistics like this all the time, but how often do we really put these things into context when it comes to our lives?

95%...

...that means that for every 100 people who lose weight, 95 of them gain it right back again.

Now, most reasonable people (and even a few unreasonable ones) would agree that there's something seriously wrong here. Yet for decades, the weight loss industry has been recycling and repackaging the same quick fix diet solutions that yield no long term results.

And for some reason people are STILL BUYING!

Now, I'm not a conspiracy theorist. However, I am aware (just as you probably are) that it is possible for the majority of the general public to "know" something that's completely untrue, ineffective, and yes, even dangerous.

Just think about the Third Reich under the leadership of Adolf Hitler.... an entire nation gone insane. In fact, there were even mature and well educated people under Hitler who were driven to violence, hatred and murder.

You see, it's not what we know that really hurts us....it's that we "know" what's not true.

Is it possible to know, believe and live by things which aren't true? Of course, all we have to be is be unconscious to the fact that what we "know" is wrong and we'll keep right on believing it, living by it and getting the same results over and over and over.

This is the way most of us live our lives, unconscious of our own habits and beliefs; blindly repeating the same actions over and over, while expecting different results. The only way to put a stop to this is to wake up and accept that something needs to change....and that's what this book is all about.

Waking up skinny begins with waking up. That said; let me ask you again...

What if your current beliefs about dieting were guaranteed to KEEP you from ever becoming thin? How ready would you be to do a total recall of your beliefs and your behaviors in regard to getting thin? Better yet, how would you feel about making the change to something which was positive and effective?

How ready would you be to hop out of bed with excitement and get moving when the "wake up call" that shows you the EXACT road map to making this happen showed up?

Picture this: you're lost, driving around in the middle of nowhere. After about an hour, you come to a gas station and stop to ask for directions. As you are speaking to the attendant, you spread your map to show him where your destination is and he looks at you, pauses, and then says:

"Oh, well that's the wrong map. No wonder you're lost."

Sure, you may be disappointed or even angry...but how ready would you be to get a hold of the right map?

Well, hold that thought for just a moment...

FIRST, A YOU TURN

I'm offering you permission to do two things right now: First, forgive yourself.

Forgive yourself for being overweight and even for "failing" to succeed in doing something about it.

It's not your fault.

Why not?

Because fault requires choice and choice requires knowledge of options.

Think about it you weren't born knowing how to read, write or drive a car. You had to learn just like everyone else. In the same way, you weren't born knowing how to take care of your body; and stay healthy and thin. You had to learn that, too.

Here's the problem...

Most of us have learned about dieting and nutrition from advertising. Those of us who didn't learn from advertising probably learned from someone else who did. This advertising comes from companies who are interested in selling more food by making it cheaper to package, produce and market; and more appealing to the taste buds.

Not exactly things that encourage healthy eating habits. However, for most people this means our options for staying thin and healthy are based on this knowledge, and therefore, we simply aren't aware that there are any other choices available to us. This means it's not your fault.

However, once you learn the material in this book it's going to become something else: your responsibility. Responsibility means you have both the option, and the power, to change.

This book gives you both.

The second thing I'm offering you permission to do is get mad.

It's ok to be mad. In fact, since we are going to turn that anger into motivation and initiative, I encourage you to get mad.

Why?

Because most people who are frustrated with their weight are so burned-out that they have nowhere else to turn their anger and drive, but inwards. They are angry with themselves because they didn't have enough willpower, motivation or drive to "make it happen." However, it doesn't matter how much drive and ambition you have, if you have the wrong map you are certain to NEVER reach your destination.

You'll only burn yourself out trying.

However, once you get a hold of the right map you'll have a renewed sense of confidence that your initiative and motivation will no longer be in vain. You can turn all of your anger, passion, motivation and desire into positive action.

You can stop feeling at fault and start being responsible.

You see, of all the people I know personally who have reinvented their bodies and their lives, not one of them had it handed to them on a silver platter. They all decided what they wanted and then they worked, studied, found mentors and went after what they wanted with everything that they had. They become responsible to change and that made all of the difference.

It starts with making a total recall in regard to what you "know" about healthy weight loss....

CHANGE ONLY CHANGES WHEN YOU CHANGE

Right about now, you're probably wondering what this "map" actually is.

It starts with your self-image.

To clarify, let me tell you a story I heard a while back that made a real impact on me...

A scorpion is sitting by the river looking at the other side and thinking "I wonder how I could get over there since I can't swim." Then he notices that there are frogs swimming easily across river, and he has an idea.

"Excuse me Mr. Frog," the scorpion says approaching one of them, "I would like to get over to the other side of the river and I see that you frogs are having no problem doing so. Would you mind if I rode on your back and crossed over to the other side with you?"

"Gasp," the frog responded, "I'm sorry, Mr. Scorpion, but I can't let you on my back. You'll sting me and I will die before I reach the other side. That's what scorpions do, you kill frogs."

"Don't be silly, Mr. Frog," the scorpion replied. "If I do that I'll drown and die with you."

The frog thought about it for a second, and since it made *logical* sense he agreed to grant the scorpion his request.

However, as the frog was about halfway across the river the scorpion jammed his stinger into the frog's back.

"Agh! The frog yelled, "What did you do that for? Now I am going to die and you'll drown before you reach the other side!"

"Because Mr. Frog," the scorpion explained, "I'm a scorpion and that's what scorpions do: we kill frogs."

You see, it is in our nature to behave in a way that is consistent with what we believe about ourselves. This belief is our self-image and our self-image is at the root of our identity and behavior.

For example, have you ever known someone who had a gift or a talent that they didn't use? Chances are it was because they didn't believe in the talent or even acknowledge it.

It was not a part of their self-image or identity.

How about someone who was attractive or even thin but who didn't believe it? Were their actions (for better or worse) based more on how attractive or thin they really were or on what they actually *believed* about themselves?

You see, it's your self-image that controls your consistent actions. In fact, Zig Ziglar said; "You cannot perform in a manner that is inconsistent with the way you see yourself."

For an example of this, just look at the way people act on the first few dates or even the first few weeks of starting a new job. With enough conscious effort, just about anyone can keep up the façade....for a time. However, eventually their actions will snap back to something which is more consistent with their subconscious beliefs about who they are.

This is the reason why 95% of people who *force* the change of weight loss are not able to keep up the lifestyle needed to maintain that healthy weight once they reach it.

Most people have no clue as to the unbelievable power that resides in them and how they can tap into nature's intelligence....especially when it comes to their health. Even successful people who have changed their bodies so dramatically you would swear they were another person (or half the person they used to be!) don't fully understand the cause of their success. They can tell you *what* they do, but as soon as you try to put it into practice you can't help but feel that something is missing.

That something is the self-image which drives all of your consistent actions.

Waking up skinny is about doing one thing and one thing only: making you consciously aware of your ability to change your habits by changing your subconscious beliefs about who you are.

This is what sets this book apart from 95% of the dieting programs on the market.

Which side of this statistic do you want to be on?

Think about it *everyone* wants success in life....whether it be success with money, relationships or health. We *all* want to feel energized, to have a sexy, fit body; and to feel great about the way that we look.

However most dieters spend their entire life chasing diet after diet, reading book after book, listening to fitness guru after fitness guru, and yet, they lose weight only to gain it back.

Again....95%

What does this mean?

It's a reminder that doing the same things over and over while expecting different results is the definition of insanity. It means that in regard to effective weight loss, the majority of people have gone insane.

You see, success can be either incredibly elusive or it can be incredibly abundant. The difference lies in having the right mindset and the right know-how....the *right map*. This book is going to teach you how to change your habits, beliefs, and the way you identify yourself, so that you can have the body you've always wanted.

It all starts with changing what you believe about yourself. So to begin with...

MAKE IT ABOUT YOU

No one will ever care about your success as much as you do....nor should they.

This means that no matter how this change is going to benefit others in your life, make sure that it's still about you. It's your body; it's the only one you'll ever have, and ultimately, it's your responsibility....and that's a good thing.

This means it's important for you to go into this with your own definition of what it means to enjoy true success. Success means something different to each person and most of the time we only get excited about what it means to us.

Here, let's give it a shot.....

Wikipedia describes the definition of success as: *1) a level of social status 2) achievement of an objective/goal 3) the opposite of failure.*

Not much to go by and definitely not very exciting.

Success to you may be getting back into those "skinny jeans" without the help of two strong men and seventeen jars of Vaseline. It might mean getting up a flight of stairs without feeling like you have a dead sumo wrestler sitting on your chest when you reach the top. It might just mean feeling great about summer coming and looking sexy in your new bathing suit.

The point is that if you are going to get emotionally involved and really get your butt in gear, your success has to mean something to you. Again, it's your body and no one will ever care about it (nor should they) more than you.

I personally define success as having fulfillment in my life. Ask anyone else and they'll likely give you another definition. No matter what, creating true success does not have to be trying, exhausting or draining. It can simply unfold like so many other miraculous creations in our universe.

The difference lies in the meaning of your goal. The more personal your goal is to you, the more you will own it. The more natural the process will be of pursuing and attracting it and the happier you will be when you reach it.

The benefit to those around you will be having someone in their life who is healthy, successful and inspiring to be around.

I'm guessing that sounds like a fair trade. So, before we get started.

MAKE THE MOST OF THIS BOOK

Most people spend more time planning a vacation than they spend planning their life and health. Don't be one of those people. Don't just read this book and put it away, hoping things will change. If you do not change, nothing will change. Own this book and let it change you for the better.

To get the most out of this book, read it once through first. This will help you to get a feel for the process of applying these principals before you put them into action.

While you are reading, make this book yours: underline, highlight or even create "dog-ears" on the pages that contain any bit of information you feel is important to you. Make notes in the margin about things you want to put into action; squeeze every ounce of juice out of it that you possibly can.

Once you are finished, go back and review your notes, and the pages that you "dog-eared" or highlighted, again and again. Every time you read it, you'll remind yourself of what you need to do in order to get from where you are now to you where you want to be.

Repetition is the key to learning, internalizing and applying something so that you can get solid results. The more you read and internalize these concepts, the more familiarity you'll associate with doing so; and the more natural part of your thinking and being they will become.

As you start to see results, you'll start to feel pleasure and begin associating that pleasure with learning and taking positive action. This feeling of pleasure will build and accelerate into raw and unstoppable momentum that will catapult you toward your goal.

You will change, and as you do, so will your actions and your life. Let's get started…

2

A Look Under the Hood:

HOW YOUR BRAIN IS WIRED

THE TWO SIDES OF THE COIN

Stop me if you've heard this one:

"I know I should but _______"

Without even filling in the blank, surely you're familiar with this pattern. You know what to do, you just aren't doing it. The reason why matters very little, since most of the time it's no more than an excuse. In fact, let's take this for a test run…

Right now, stop what you're doing and write down ONE thing that you could stop doing today that is causing you to remain overweight.

Got it? Good.

Now write down ONE thing you could start doing that would help you LOSE weight.

Ok, so what does this mean? It means that before I start giving you a whole lot of NEW information, we need to deal with the reason you're not using what you *already* have. If we don't address that first, I'm just giving you a bunch of new things to feel guilty about because you aren't *using* them.

Keep reading if you're with me on this….

Wouldn't you like to know the real reason you aren't using what you already know?

It's because you are not emotionally engaged with what you know.

Let me clarify...

It's been said that a single death is a tragedy and that one million

deaths is a statistic.

Consider these statistics:

- In the United States, 40 thousand people per year die in car accidents
- In the United States, a new baby is born every 10 seconds

Now try these:

- Your mother was just in a car accident and is in the ICU fighting for her life
- A new baby boy was just born to a young couple in Orlando, Fl. The baby's name is Stevie and he has his mother's eyes he seems to like the color blue.

Now as you are reading the first set of statistics, you probably don't notice much of a change in your physiology. In other words, you have little or no emotional response, because they are strictly factual. There is no emotional context in which you can identify with them.

However, as you read the second two stories, you probably noticed a response from your body, didn't you? In the same way, you can read about how over 30 million people died in the Spanish influenza outbreak of the early 20th century and have little emotional response to it.

This is not because you are insensitive; it has to do with the way that your brain is wired. You see, there are two sides of your brain.

One side, your left brain, deals simply with facts, numbers and statistics. It is the left side of your brain that processes logical information and has little or no effect on your emotional state.

However, the right side of your brain is the more creative and abstract side of your brain. However, this side of your brain speaks a different language than the logical side of your brain. This is the side of your brain that processes things in an emotional context. If you give it statistics, it can't do anything with them. You have to speak its language by giving those statistics an emotional context.

For instance, I can tell you a story about a man named Stan who died of the Spanish influenza at the age of 42. Stan was the husband of Candace and father of two children, Brian, age 11; and Alicia, age 13.

Every Sunday the family would to get dressed up and go to church together. On the way home they would stop for ice cream; Stan's favorite flavor was green mint. He would always tease his son, Brian, that if he ate too much green mint he would turn green when he grew up.

When Stan passed away Candace and the children would all sit around his favorite chair and read stories at bedtime. One night, Brian asked his mother, "Mommy, will daddy be green in heaven?"

They laughed…..then Candace sent the children to bed and cried.

You see the difference? Once you become emotionally involved in something, you begin to notice a change in your body. This is because your logical mind is one kind of intelligence in your body, and the one that has the least influence on your actions.

In other words, *knowing* something on a factual level is completely separate from knowing it on an emotional level.

So what does this mean in regard to putting your current stock of knowledge to work for you?

MORE THAN A FEELING: EMOTIONAL INTELLIGENCE AND BEYOND

We've all heard the saying, knowledge is power.

In reality, it is nothing of the sort. It's the knowledge that we put into consistent action that brings results and influences our lives.

So where is the misunderstanding about knowledge being power?

The misunderstanding lies in what it means to *know* something. As you now know, your logical intelligence holds a small fraction of your "knowability."

Picture an iceberg: the tip represents only 10% of the iceberg the other 90% is below the surface of the water. This is the natural intelligence that lies in the cells of your body. This is the part of you that the ancients referred to as "the heart."

Relax! I'm not talking about any mystical chakra work here.

What I'm talking about is in fact a sound scientific reality. Your body contains the full capacity to know things on a level that will move you to action. Once you know things on this level, the knowledge you already have becomes real and tangible because it can yield true results. This is the source of your personal power.

How does it work?

Remember that feeling you had when you read the story about Stan? What you were feeling was an electrical vibration in your physical body. This vibration of your nervous system is interpreted by your mind as an emotion.

Let's break this down on a scientific level…

If you ever get the chance to sit in a soundproof chamber, you'll actually notice two sounds. One of them will be like the sound of white noise and the other will be like a low electrical hum. These are the sounds of your physical body. The white noise sound is your blood rushing through your veins and the hum is the vibration of your nervous system.

Most of the time, these sounds are drowned out by the sounds going on around us. However, our body is still sensitive enough to feel the vibration it is in. Again, this feeling in your body is interpreted as your emotional state. In fact, anyone who has ever had a pet can tell you that their pet seems to "know" what emotional state they are in.

This does not mean that dogs and cats have a sixth sense. What it means it that their sense of hearing is keen enough to hear the vibration of your nervous system and of your blood rushing through your veins.

You see, as you become emotionally involved with an idea or piece of information, it moves your body into a vibration which is consistent with the emotional "color" of that thought this is the body preparing itself for action. If you've ever seen a martial artist posturing up before a fight, you'll notice that they literally scream out loud to get themselves revved up. This is because that scream actually sends a physical vibration through their nervous system that prepares their body for action.

In fact, advertising research is specifically designed to find out what kinds of words, sounds, pictures, colors, images, music and stories will initiate physiological responses in people; causing them to take action and buy. Advertisers have this down to such a science that they understand what will cause changes in heart rate, breathing, pupil dilation, protein release and the vibration of your nervous system.

All of these represent the intelligence which is wrapped up in the cells of your body.

Now let me ask you this...

If advertisers can use this information to get people to take action and buy their products, how might you be able to harness this power to spur yourself to positive action?

What I am referring to here is a level of learning where you engage more than just your logical mind. It's a method for becoming emotionally and physically involved in a positive idea before you ever set out to put it into practice.

Add consistency and repetition to this and these ideas will naturally move you to action and ensure positive results. Additionally, as you become involved with ideas on this level, they become part of your identity; which is the very thing that controls your consistent actions.

Now in case I made that sound really easy, let's come back down to earth…

FOUR STAGES OF LEARNING: THE SIX-INCH DROP FROM THE HEAD TO THE HEART

Surely you're aware that it is much easier to keep working at something if you understand the process that gets results. In other words, if you're running a mile it helps if you have landmarks along the way to check your progress; and to encourage you that you are actually getting somewhere.

In the same way, the process of moving an idea from logical "knowledge" to "heart" knowledge has stages. Once you understand these stages, it'll be a lot easier for you to make that six-inch drop from the head to the heart:

The following are the four stages of learning:

- Stage One: Unconsciously Incompetent
- Stage Two: Consciously Incompetent
- Stage Three: Consciously Competent
- Stage Four: Unconsciously Competent Now let's break these down…

STAGE ONE: UNCONSCIOUSLY INCOMPETENT

This is the first autopilot stage. This is when you are engaged in a negative action that has become such a habit that you are no longer aware of the fact that you are even doing it. For example, every time you smell something that might be good to eat, you automatically want to eat it. You aren't consciously aware of the fact that it is craving not actual hunger that is driving you, so you don't stop and think about what you are doing. You just think, "Gosh, I really want some buttered popcorn." And you eat.

STAGE TWO: CONSCIOUSLY INCOMPETENT

This is where you move out of autopilot and into a state of awareness that you are engaging in a negative behavior. Maybe you read a book that tells you there is a difference between hunger and cravings (hint, hint). Now, you are consciously aware that you are engaged in a negative behavior and have a choice to make: You either make a conscious decision to choose a different behavior and move to stage three or you move into a state of denial. (I'll tell you in a second how that works.) Either way, you have entered the second stage of learning, where you have an awareness of the fact that you are engaging in a negative behavior.

STAGE THREE: CONSCIOUSLY COMPETENT

This is the point where most of us fall off the tightrope on our way to stage four. This is because although we are consciously aware of what we need to do and we are actively doing it, we are still operating on a conscious and logical level. We have not made the six-inch drop from the head to the heart and become emotionally engaged with the idea or the behavior yet. Since most people are unaware of how to engage their physical intelligence in such a way, they rely strictly on willpower to get them to stage four. This is the reason 95% of people who lose weight gain it back. This is why 95% of New Year's Resolutions never make it past the second week of January. And so on and so on…

Making sense?

STAGE FOUR: UNCONSCIOUSLY COMPETENT

This is the second autopilot stage. This is the person to whom success comes to so naturally that it seems they were simply born that way. Their ability to succeed seems almost magical and we regard them as "lucky." In fact, for many people in this stage their positive behavior is so unconscious that they are completely unaware of it even when you ask them about it specifically. This is the reason why most successful people aren't able to tell you how they did it. To them, it happens as naturally as water flows downhill.

Don't you hate that?

As a teacher of personal motivation and the psychology of human behavior, I have learned to take a step back into stage two. What I have found is that as natural as stage four appears to be, it can be taught and that's why you are reading this book.

But before we move on, let's talk what you are actually up against...

THE SCIENCE OF DENIAL: YOUR RETICULAR ACTIVATION SYSTEM

You are probably wondering, *"If this is so effective, why isn't everybody doing it?"*

Well, it's because of an unseen "enemy" whose primary job is to keep you locked in Stage One: Unconscious Incompetence. However, once you know the enemy, it can become your best friend.

That enemy is denial.

You may be familiar with what Walt Kelly said, *"We have seen the enemy, and it's us."*

This doesn't mean that you are a bad person or that you have to be mad at yourself. In fact, denial is a natural defense mechanism and there's no point in feeling bad about it. It becomes negative when it keeps you from recognizing the patterns of belief and behavior that are holding you back.

However, denial isn't something you can get rid of....at least not without a lobotomy.

You see, your brain actually has a device called your Reticular Activation System or RAS. The purpose of the RAS is to filter out the billions of bits of information per second that are being absorbed by your senses, only allowing the bits of information that your mind regards as relevant.

For instance, have you ever learned a new vocabulary word and suddenly begin hearing it three or four times a week?

This means that either everyone you encountered got together and said, "*Hey, Mark knows the word antiquated now, so we can finally start using it around him!"* Or that something shifted in your mind, which caused you to start noticing that word instead of filtering it out.

Think about that one it'll come to you.

How about when you're thinking about buying a new car and you start seeing it everywhere? Your RAS is constantly filtering out the things which are not relevant to your experience or beliefs it has to.

Think about it we live in the most aggressively solicited society in history. Every second we are bombarded with ideas and information and emotional stimuli. There is simply no way that we can take it all in, let alone become emotionally involved in it. Therefore, the RAS is a defense mechanism that helps us to filter out the information which is not relevant.

Sure, it can't help you to filter out the person who runs up to you on the street and starts singing happy birthday right in your face in the key of Q minor. This is because there are certain experiences which demand your attention whether you want them to or not. However, what the RAS will do is filter and store that memory according to what is consistent with your perspectives and beliefs. How else do you think three people can give an account of an accident and come up with three different stories?

Now you know how you can be talking to someone and feeling that they just aren't "hearing" you? They may even "hear" something that you didn't say at all, as if they heard what they wanted to hear.

Give me a silent nod if you're with me on this…

Considering this, it's easy to see why your perceptions and beliefs regarding healthy weight loss and self-image have to be as much a part of your transformation as your eating habits.

The good news is that you can program your RAS to filter out the things which might distract you from achieving your goals.

That's certainly better than a lobotomy, right?

Now, before we start to turn this thing around, let's talk about the second dynamic of your inner autopilot...

THE SCIENCE OF AUTOPILOT: YOUR PSYCHO-CYBERNETIC MECHANISM

You are getting very sleepy....

Okay, relax I'm not trying to put you in a trance....yet.

What most people aren't aware of is that all of us are in a trance of some sort. It's called your subconscious conditioning. Again, this is a defense mechanism and it's not necessarily a "bad" thing. The only thing that makes your conditioning bad or good is the behaviors which it initiates in you.

We call this conditioning autopilot, and it is controlled by both your RAS and your Psycho-Cybernetic Mechanism.

Think about it this way...

You set your car on cruise control at 50mph. Now you can step on the gas for a few seconds and make the car go faster or you can step on the brakes and slow down. However, as soon as you disengage, your speed is going to level out at 50mph again.

Your Psycho-Cybernetic Mechanism is like cruise control.

It controls the subconscious image which you have of yourself (remember, your self-image is not the same as your true identity). Instead, it is the image of yourself that is most consistent with your perceptions and beliefs about who you are, what you deserve, and what you are capable of. It's also the very thing that controls your actions, for better or worse.

For example, if your Psycho-Cybernetic Mechanismhas your inner cruise control set according to being "lazy, unmotivated, ugly and overweight," your Psycho-Cybernetic Mechanism will do whatever it can to make sure that your outer reality is consistent with your inner self-image.

You can step on the gas and force change by sheer force of will. However, when your physical results start to change and your Psycho-Cybernetic Mechanism recognizes that they are not consistent with your inner perception, it will begin to reset your behavior in order to make your outer reality consistent with your inner reality.

This is why 95% of people who lose weight gain it back. This is why people who are living paycheck to paycheck get a pay raise but increase their spending until they are living paycheck to paycheck again. This is why the majority of lottery winners end up broke within a few years. This is why people who are used to being in abusive relationships sabotage their own happiness as soon as an opportunity for a better relationship comes along.

Does this concern you?

Does it make you angry, fearful, or perhaps even excited?

I hope it does. In fact, the more emotionally engaged you are right now, the better. You see, my goal here is to jolt you out of stage one and into stage two by getting you emotionally involved with the idea of positive change. Once we get there, we can work on programming your RAS and Psycho-Cybernetic Mechanism so that they'll propel you in the direction of your greatest dreams.

How is this possible?

Let me put it this way: if you have been conditioned to be overweight you can also be conditioned to be thin...

GOOD VIBRATIONS: TUNING INTO THE NEW YOU

You may have heard about the difference between the subconscious mind and the conscious mind. But what you may not be aware of is the role that each one plays in your thinking process and in your life.

Without getting into all of the theories about the subconscious mind, let me just say this: your Reticular Activation System, your Psycho-

Cybernetic Mechanism, and your emotional intelligence are all functions of your subconscious mind. As you can see, they have the greatest influence over your consistent behaviors.

Although you are not consciously in control of these functions, you can use conscious processes to program them and therefore align your habits and beliefs with what you really want. This is the Consciously Competent stage of learning, and with enough consistency and perseverance you can move yourself from this stage to the Subconsciously Competent stage.

Once you move into this stage, your subconscious mind begins to create a vibration or "energy" that is in harmony with whatever you need to create the physical equivalent of your thought. (Your dog may even notice a difference).

As you consciously choose the thoughts you want, you start to impress those thoughts on your subconscious being. Over time, a new more powerful program is created. You reprogram your internal computer to work in harmony with your desires, instead of against them.

And then...

These subconscious functions will work just as hard, and just as stubbornly, to move you toward habits that will make you thin, as it is now working to keep you fat. Your Reticular Activation System will protect you from the influences which are designed to make you overweight and your Psycho-Cybernetic Mechanism will take over so that you do not constantly have to force change by sheer willpower.

Your efforts and motivation to get and to stay thin will happen just as naturally as the grass grows and water flows downhill.

I'm guessing that sounds pretty good.

Now, I imagine this is giving you the inspiration to face the uphill battle ahead with the hope and determination that you and I both know you already possess.

So let's get this show on the road...

3

To Believe

OR NOT TO BELIEVE

To be or not to be.....that is...

....well, actually it's not the question.

The question is this: to believe or not to believe.

No matter who you are or what you are capable of, your beliefs about yourself are all that really make a difference in your life. You can have all the talent in the world and the only talent you'll use and benefit from is the talent that you believe you have. You can be outwardly attractive, but you'll only carry yourself in a manner that is consistent with how attractive you believe you are. Even the relationships and possessions you are able to acquire and keep in life are determined by your level of belief in yourself.

Yes, we have been here before, haven't we? But there is a reason why I'm repeating this: it's because of the way beliefs are formed.

Did you know that if you tell a person something often enough and loud enough for a long enough period of time, their subconscious mind will believe it as truth? Your only defense against this is the filter of your conscious mind. However, if the conscious mind is not alert and actively involved in filtering out information, the subconscious mind stores that information without questioning its accuracy or logic.

Just think about the last time you were unconscious...what were you doing? You were, weren't you? You know, you walk out your front door to go to work and there's an Olympic-sized swimming pool full of peanut butter between you and your car. Meanwhile, there's a synchronized swim team of electric eels in the pool, so swimming is not an option.

You're going to be late to work! What are you going to do?

You might be laughing right now, but just think about the last time you had this kind of dream. You were probably freaking out about getting to work on time, weren't you? This is because your subconscious mind believes anything, whether it's real, unreal, or downright absurd. Without the filter of your conscious mind, you can develop beliefs and perceptions that are completely irrational and even imaginary. Thank goodness for the conscious rational mind, right?

Well, hold on for just a moment there. The problem is that the conscious mind is directly influenced by the things that you believe. Our consistent thoughts and behaviors are determined by our beliefs, while the logical mind is used to defend and support those beliefs. For example, have you ever seen someone do something completely irrational, but they had some complex rationalization to support it?

Sure, we've all seen this and we've all done it...myself included.

This is because we make decisions based on our deeply-rooted emotional convictions and seek to justify them logically.

The problem with this is that belief is a matter of perception, not reality. There are things that are true in spite of what you believe about them and there are things that are false in spite of what you believe.

In other words: it is possible for a person's beliefs to be out of sync with the truth.

How does this happen?

Well, our deepest rooted beliefs are formed before our conscious mind develops the cognitive abilities to sort the trash from the treasure. By the time it develops this ability, the conscious mind serves the purpose of defending and supporting its own beliefs.

Think of it like this: when you make cookies you start out with lumpy dough and you can make it into any shape you want to. This is much like the condition of your mind when you're young. However, after about 45 minutes in the oven you've got a solid cookie and changing its shape is much more difficult.

In the same way, your beliefs are formed when you lack the capacity to sort what is positive from what is negative. This is how your unconscious negative habits and beliefs are formed.

The good news is that unlike the baked cookie, it is possible to reshape your beliefs.

First, let's have a look at how negative beliefs are formed...

CONDITIONED RESPONSE AND BEING OVERWEIGHT

Does the name Pavlov ring a bell?

Ivan Pavlov was a scientist who conducted a series of experiments about the way beliefs and perceptions cause conditioned responses. To summarize, he rang a bell every time he fed the subject of the experiment, his dog. Eventually the dog came to associate the ringing of the bell with feeding time. Whenever the bell was rung, the dog would come running with his mouth salivating.

The dog had come to believe that the sound of the bell equaled food, so he acted accordingly. Now I know what you might be thinking you are not a dog. However, the human mind is also wired to associate specific stimuli with beliefs, whether the two are related or not.

For example, you remember the cowboy from the Marlboro cigarette commercials? What in the world do cowboys have to do with cigarettes?

Nothing.

So why did Marlboro use a cowboy in their advertising? Because Marlboro was mainly a brand smoked by women at the time and Marlboro wanted to market their product to men. The cowboy was used the same way that the ringing of the bell was used in Pavlov's experiment. Only this time the objective was for people to associate Marlboro cigarettes with being a rough and tough "man's man."

Did it work?

Well, we may not be dogs, but all you have to do is look at the results.

The human mind is wired for the conditioned response there is no way around this. However, there is a way to use the conditioned response to your advantage. You do this by building associations that will lead to positive conditioned responses.

Maybe you can't teach an old dog a new trick...but you are not a dog. You have the power to change your negative belief patterns, to change your conditioned response, and to change your life.

This begins with changing the beliefs that have caused you to be overweight...

THE BORN IDENTITY: HOW YOUR SELF-IMAGE IS FORMED

Okay, so now we get down to the core of the issue. Your selfimage is your identity and the driving force of all your habits and behaviors. Your self-image is based more on your beliefs about who you are and what you are capable of.

Don't miss that, it was good.

Want to become more than who you are right now and change your life as a result? Change what you believe about who you are, what you deserve and what you are capable of it will change everything.

It begins with understanding how your current beliefs about yourself were formed. While there are many contributing factors, there is one that makes almost all of the difference:

It's the stories you tell yourself about who you are.

Remember that a story has the emotional context to make a true impression on your mind and on your nervous system. This is how your beliefs about yourself are formed.

Of course you don't sit down and read yourself a bedtime story... or do you?

Think about this: when you think about the condition of your body, do you see yourself as a fat person? Do you talk to yourself like an overweight person with no self-control and an unattractive body? Do you see yourself as someone who lacks the discipline and the motivation to stick with your commitment to get thin?

When you mess up and break a diet, do you punish yourself with stories about how you are hopelessly addicted to eating the wrong foods? These are the stories that you tell yourself, and they are shaping your beliefs about who you are and what you are capable of.

The easiest way to recognize the stories that you are telling yourself is to listen to the way you talk to yourself. Yes, we all do this…not just crazy people.

You may not always be saying, "Mark, you are a big, fat slob," to yourself round the clock, but if you begin to pay attention, you'll realize that there is a monologue going on just about every moment you are awake. This is the act of becoming consciously aware of the belief patterns that are shaping your self-image and your life.

Most of the time our inner monologue starts out as someone else speaking to us….a parent, a teacher, a friend or even popular advertising. However, as these voices become more and more familiar in our memory we forget that they aren't ours. We adopt them and they become the inner monologue that shapes our beliefs.

This is how we become either wired for weight gain or weight loss…

ARE YOU WIRED FOR WEIGHT GAIN?

You know there is only one thing worse for a kid than eating vegetables: eating cold vegetables.

If you're like most people, it probably took you a long time to figure this one out. You know how it works: you eat everything on your plate but your lima beans and sit there and stare while they slowly form ice caps.

Of course, you had to finish them….you HAD to. After all, you need to finish all of the food on your plate if you want dessert. After all, with all the starving people in the world you should never let food go to waste. Not to mention the fact that your mother slaved over a hot stove to make you dinner and you don't want to disappoint or upset her.

Translation: if you don't eat everything on your plate you are bad, ungrateful and make mommy very unhappy. Now to your adult mind this might sound absurd, but we're talking about a belief that was formed a long time ago. In other words, the cookie dough has been shaped, baked in the oven at 400o degrees and set out to cool.

Whether or not these beliefs make sense to you now is not the point. The point is that they're a reality now and a major contributing factor to your being overweight. Think about this: how often do you actually leave food on your plate? Sure, you may not be saying, "Gee, I'd better finish everything on my plate or ______."

The behavior has now become so subconscious that you no longer think about it, you just respond as you always have.

When you think about it, we are exposed to all kinds of messages that encourage overeating. Just have a look at some of these:

"Get your own bag." "One just isn't enough."

"Crunch all you want, we'll make more." "Life is short, snack often."

"You deserve a break today." "Indulge yourself."

"Have it your way."

When you think about it, all of these are based on the "if it feels good, do it" philosophy. Now there is nothing wrong with getting pleasure out of eating, but if pleasure becomes the primary focus of eating that's when we get into trouble. These cute little taglines suddenly become the stories that we tell ourselves, and as these stories become beliefs, they create a specific conditioned response: overeating.

Pretty good marketing strategy on the part of the food companies, but not so good for your personal health. Now, in case you don't think these messages are getting into your psyche, just try filling in some of these blanks:

"Melts in your ______, not in your ______."

"Pepsi, the choice of a new ______."

"It's a good for the great of ______."

"Nike: Just ______."

This is pretty impressive when sometimes we can't remember what our spouse said to us five minutes ago. Whether you believe these things to be true when you first hear them is not what matters. If you have these things memorized, it means they've gotten into your subconscious mind.

The most important thing to realize here is that the subconscious is the most impressionable when a person is young. Food marketers have been under fire recently for aggressively marketing to kids. According to the Institute of Medicine, $10 billion a year is spent marketing foods to children. McDonalds with their Happy Meals (fried crap with a toy!), Sponge Bob Mac and Cheese, Dora The Explorer cookies…I could go on and on. Just about every sugary cereal that you see has some kind of cartoon character on it.

These food manufactures come into your home while your kids are watching their favorite TV show. This makes it almost impossible to walk down a grocery isle with your child. It makes it even harder to instruct them about good nutrition. Food manufacturers also used product placement to place their sugar and saturated fat packed foods right in your children's line of sight. This is based on the concept that "eye level is buy level." Even if you don't buy these things for your kids, these images get into their subconscious minds, and over a period of time, something called "brand loyalty" is built.

This brand loyalty is what causes adults to spend up to 30% more simply for foods with branded packaging, in spite of the fact that the ingredients are no different from those with generic packaging. And it doesn't end with marketing sugary foods to kids. Credit card companies who understand brand loyalty are now sponsoring educational toys for use in public schools which contain fake credit cards with their brand logo. Is it any wonder why more and more college age adults are filing for bankruptcy? Or why the obesity rate among children under ten is increasing so dramatically?

I believe the same way we saw cigarette ads almost completely banned over the last 50 years we'll see the same with advertising to children, but until then, the best line of defense is a good education. The purpose of this education must be more than the mere accumulation of information and knowledge; it also requires proper conditioning of the subconscious mind.

Remember, the subconscious mind can't tell what's real from what's not real. That's why irrational dreams can still evoke very real fear and anxiety. Not only that, but your reticular activation system filters your experience according to what is consistent with your beliefs and perceptions.

In other words, your beliefs shape your view of the world, your self-image and your conditioned responses, whether they make logical sense or not. This is how you become subconsciously wired for weight gain. In order to lose weight and KEEP it off, you have to get rid of the subconscious conditioning which has made you this way. You must deliberately replace it with beliefs and conditioning that will make your body want to be thin.

This means changing the stories that you tell yourself...

AUTOSUGGESTION: YOUR COMPLETE MONOLOGUE MAKEOVER

Changing the stories that you tell yourself is really as easy as it sounds.

The problem is that if you've been telling yourself the wrong stories for years and years, it's going to take some time for the new stories to have an impact. This requires an understanding of what ingredients will make a powerful and emotionally charged story that will leave a lasting impression on your subconscious mind.

The technical term for this is autosuggestion and it's accomplished through the application of positive affirmations. This is quite a bit more than just positive thinking; there is a specific formula that

your affirmations need to follow in order to be effective in altering your beliefs and your self-image.

Now, I'm going to do more here than just give you the formula I'm going to explain the principles behind each step of building empowering affirmations. There are two reasons for doing this:

- People usually work harder at something when they understand why they are doing it.
- If you can get the principles of autosuggestion down, you can apply them to other areas of your life.

Here we go....

First, there are three kinds of learning styles: in order for you to get the most out of your autosuggestion, it's important for you to know your personal learning style. This way you can customize the practice of your affirmations so they have the most powerful effect on your subconscious mind.

Here are the three learning styles:

- Visual
- Auditory
- Kinesthetic

Visual means that visual stimuli have the strongest effect on your mind and make it easier for you to learn something. Auditory means that the things you *hear* have the strongest impression and kinesthetic means that you are a "hands-on" learner and internalize things you become physically engaged in.

Now, of course using all three of these kinds of stimuli will make the strongest impression on anyone. However, knowing your personal learning style will help you get your affirmations laserfocused and break past the barriers of your old beliefs even faster.

How do you know your learning style? When you're learning something new are you more likely to want to see pictures or hear the instructions? Are you more likely to read a book or do you prefer to listen to an audio book? Are you more hands-on when it comes to learning or do you need to see something done first?

This may take some time...and if you are not sure right now which style you are, don't worry. I'll show you how to apply each one to practicing your affirmations and you'll find your learning style that way. But first, let's look at the formula for effective affirmations:

The easiest way to remember how to create and use affirmations is with this simple acronym:

S.P.E.A.K.

- Specific
- Present
- Emotional
- Affirmative
- Keep it up

We are going to use an example for creating an affirmation for getting to your ideal body weight. However, I encourage you to use this formula to create at least three of your own. The more personal your affirmations are the more effective they will be...

SPECIFIC

Your affirmations must be specific in order to be effective. The subconscious mind does not do well with generalities and vague instructions. Remember, it has no ability to analyze information, so generalities tell it nothing. For example; "I want to lose weight" or "I want to make more money" or "I want to reach my ideal weight," is too vague for the subconscious.

Instead, be specific about what you want. How much weight are you going to lose? What is your precise, ideal weight? How much money do you want to make a week?

As an example, let's say that your ideal body weight is 130 lbs. with 12% body fat.

PRESENT

The subconscious mind experiences everything in the present…In other words, when you think about something that happened in the past, your subconscious relives the experience as if it were happening right now. If your affirmations are always referring to *another* time (past or future) then it won't internalize the affirmation as being true.

For example, if you say, "I will weigh 130 lbs….." You are telling your subconscious that you are NOT at your ideal weight and this is the belief that it will act from. However, if your subconscious begins to believe you are at your ideal weight, it will adjust your behavior to be consistent with that condition.

Continuing our example, your affirmation would now read: "I am now at my ideal body weight of 130 lbs. and my body fat percentage is 12%."

EMOTIONAL

In order to truly internalize a belief, you have to become emotionally involved with it. Remember, your emotions set up a vibration in your body that prepares your body for action. If you are not emotionally involved in your affirmation, it won't have any effect on your physiology or your actions; and you'll eventually feel that you are lying to yourself when you say it.

In order to get emotionally involved with what you are affirming, you must give it an emotionally charged context. For example; how are you going to feel when you are finally at your ideal weight and 12% body fat? Excited? Sexy? Content? Confident? Proud? Include these words in your affirmation:

"I am so confident and content to be at my ideal body weight of 130 lbs. and 12% body fat."

AFFIRMATIVE

This may very well be the MOST important step to creating an effective affirmation: make it affirmative! In other words, affirm what you want instead of what you don't want. If you say, "I don't want to be overweight" or "I am not overweight anymore" or "I need to stop ______," you are not talking about what you want, you're talking about what you don't want.

Remember that your subconscious can't reason (this includes deductive reasoning and the process of elimination). In other words, if you tell it what you don't want, it has no reference with which to determine what you DO want. Not to mention that as soon as you say, "I don't want ______," your subconscious draws up an image of whatever you put in the blank.

Don't believe me?

Try this: don't picture a red circus tent.

What are you thinking about? The subconscious believes whatever is the most present experience. If you keep drawing up images of chocolate cheesecake by saying, "I need to stop eating chocolate cheesecake," guess what is going to have the strongest influence on your subconscious?

So avoid words like don't, not, can't, won't, quit, stop, etc.; anything that is associated with what you DON'T want. Instead, ask yourself what you DO want and focus on that.

Now, since our example is already affirmative, let's move on to the last step.

"I am so confident and content to be at my ideal body weight of 130 lbs. and 12% body fat."

KEEP IT UP

I can't stress this step enough: You MUST keep telling yourself the right stories by using your affirmations on a consistent basis.

For how long? Well, let me put it this way: autosuggestion is like taking a shower; a little bit a day is all you need, but if you slack off you'll start to stink.

In other words, five to fifteen minutes a day is just fine. However, you can't do three hours and ride that out for the entire week. You also can't do a crash course and get rid of all your negative beliefs by doing 48 solid hours in one weekend.

You must do it every day and there is no need to kill yourself…fifteen minutes is just fine. Just keep it up and make it a lifelong habit….even after you are at your ideal weight. Trust me, once you see the results you won't want to stop.

Now, you may be wondering about how to apply these to your personal learning style. As I mentioned, using all three is great. However, if you really want to throw some gasoline on the fire, here is what you need to do:

- For visual learners

  Write your affirmations down and read them out loud while looking at them. Even if you get them memorized, keep reading them. Other options are creating a collage with pictures of healthy foods and thin and happy people. If you have a great imagination you can even close your eyes and imagine yourself thin. Give yourself as much visual stimuli as possible to create an impression on your subconscious mind.

- For auditory learners

  In addition to speaking your affirmations out loud, record them in your own voice and listen to them. You can put them on your iPod® or burn them to a CD and listen to them in your car. Just be sure that you are paying attention to them and that you are feeling the emotional states you will experience when your affirmation is true.

  The following are two places you can go online and record your own audio programs. www.prvsoft.com and http://vocaroo.com/

- For kinesthetic learners

  For hands-on learners, the best option is the physical act of writing out your affirmations by hand. Writing is great because it engages the visual, auditory and kinesthetic faculties. However, for handson people it is the best way to become physically involved in your affirmations. In addition, hands-on learners can practice pushing their plates away from them while the plate still has food on it.

  The motivational expert, Tony Robbins, actually sat down and practiced pushing his plate away over and over, while working himself into a peak state of emotional pleasure. This was a key contributing factor to his losing 30 pounds.

Whatever you are doing, be sure that your affirmations are sticking to EVERY principle in the SPEAK approach and that you do everything possible to make them personal. As you do this, you'll find that you are taking more ownership of them and they will become a part of your beliefs and life.

Now, in order for this to really work we've got to do something first…

MAKING YOUR OWN WAKE UP CALL

Steven MR Covey tells a story where he went to the beach with his family one summer when his daughter was still very young. As he was getting ready to go into the water, he took his T-shirt off. When his young daughter saw this, she said, "Whoa Daddy, you have a big tummy."

Ouch.

Why does it sting so much when we get this kind of candid and ontarget feedback from someone else? Because in spite of the fact that we know it to be true, we have such a thick wall of rationalizations and beliefs that support our lifestyle that we aren't able to be objective. We have ourselves so well fooled that when we realize we're not fooling those around us, it hits us like a ton of bricks.

This is a good thing. It jolts us out of the Unconsciously Incompetent stage and forces us to face what's real. This is when we become consciously aware of our negative conditioning. Another example was someone I knew who lost over one hundred pounds in a little over a year. This was someone who had been overweight for the majority of their adult life.

However, the reality of their condition didn't hit them until one day when they tried to get onto a hanging roller coaster and found that the restraining device would not lock down over their torso. They had to be moved to a special seat which had been made for overweight people. Although the people attending the ride were pleasant and professional, the occasion ended up being a wakeup call.

"*Until then, I really didn't realize that I was seriously overweight,*" he said.

Again, this is because they were too immersed in their inner conditioning to see the reality of their outer condition.

You may have heard the proverb, "There are three great mysteries: water to a fish, air to a bird, and to a man...himself." In other words, the most familiar things around us are often the things we know the least. We take them for granted and even assume that we understand them...so we never take a closer look.

But it's time to wake up.

Before you go on to the next chapter, sit down and create a list of all the things being overweight is doing to your life and how it affects your relationships, energy level, self-esteem, ability to enjoy life, health, and yes, even your longevity. This might make you feel horrible, but that's a good thing...the purpose is to jolt you out of your comfort zone and force you to confront the reality of where you are now. Don't worry, you aren't going to stay there...but in order to get to the place you really want to, you must pass this way.

Go ahead and do it right now I'll see you on the next page.

4

Identifying the

SIX COMMON DENOMINATORS

He was the first man to run a four-minute mile. Before he did this, everyone said that it couldn't be done; obviously they were wrong. And can you guess what happened after that? Several people followed Roger Bannister by running a four-minute mile. Today, it's hardly considered a big deal among professional runners.

How about Chuck Yeager? He was the first airplane pilot who managed to travel faster than the speed of sound. Once he accomplished this breakthrough, dozens of other people followed in his footsteps by breaking the sound barrier themselves.

I could go on, but the point is that people have a curious capability of accomplishing great things once they realize it is possible to do so. There are a couple of reasons for this, but the main reason is that people who dare to push past the boundaries of what is "impossible" leave the rest of us with no excuses. They also encourage us and give us hope; if they can do it, maybe we can do it as well.

That is the first purpose of this chapter.

The other thing we are going to do is to identify the six common denominators required to achieve a healthy lifestyle:

- **A moment of awakening:** hitting rock bottom, feeling desperate, being inspired by an insight or epiphany or a combination of the two.
- **Taking responsibility:** acknowledging that only you can change your life and taking responsibility instead of blaming circumstances and other people.

- **Taking Action:** taking action whether you are ready or not, instead of waiting for that elusive "someday."
- **Changing inner dialogue and image:** see yourself as a positive and motivated person, instead of as lazy and overweight.
- **Developing self-respect:** developing a healthy view of yourself and being happy with who you are.
- **Practicing consistency:** committing yourself to a perpetual lifestyle based on constant improvement and devotion to personal growth.

To further illustrate these principles, let's look at a few real-life case studies from some of my previous clients. As we look at these examples, we're going to cover how each of the six common denominators played a role in their success.

SHE LOST 47 POUNDS AND KEPT IT OFF

CAROL BEFORE

CAROL AFTER

Carol from Tennessee was retired from the United States Air Force after 28 years of service. She had grown up in a household where everyone had a great metabolism and was able to eat without gaining excessive weight. In fact, Carol said that snacking on sugary foods was fairly common, and that her family did a lot of southern-style cooking, which consisted of lots of greasy, fatty, fried foods. In regard to physical activity, playing outside and casual walks around the neighborhood to visit friends was pretty much all there was to it.

However, like most people, as Carol got older she realized she was busting out of the size 10 that used to fit her comfortably. Not only that, she was married to a man who was very active and in good shape and was finding it difficult to keep up with him. On top of all that, she had retired to a hobby farm where she was doing dog training, and working to take care of 60 acres of land; something she had little energy for because she was overweight.

Like most overweight people, Carol didn't realize she had a problem until she noticed that her clothes did not fit like they used to. Like most people trying to lose weight, Carol tried numerous fad diets: the Atkins diet, something she called the "stinky salad diet," diets that promised she would lose 10 pounds for the weekend, and other cookie-cutter solutions. However, her greatest weight loss with these methods was 17 pounds, which she later gained back.

According to Carol, she had no willpower or impulse control when it came to eating. If she wanted to have a few Girl Scout cookies, she would sit down and eat the entire sleeve. If she wanted some chips, she would sit down and eat half a bag or more.

Carol said her moment of awakening came when she realized she might have to use a pair of pliers to pull up the zipper on her size 10 dress. That was when she decided to attend one of our weightloss seminars. She began to take responsibility for changing her life. She devoted herself to being more active and changing the way she thought about food. As a result, she eventually reached the point where she didn't have the cravings she had formerly had for foods like chips or chocolate. "The cravings just aren't there anymore," she said, "The chocolate isn't screaming out my name like it used to."

In addition to taking action and changing things, she began to see herself as a healthy, active person who had greater self-control and willpower. She had once seen herself as a couch potato who didn't feel like doing anything, but as she became more active, she was less likely to want to "veg out" on the couch. She paid attention to food labels and controlling her portions, and she began to sleep better.

Most importantly, Carol learned the value of constant improvement for sustaining her success. She said the very moment she felt she was starting to slide she would get back into the reinforcement materials she obtained at our seminars. She realized, just as you will, that they were the key she needed to cultivate new habits and support a healthy lifestyle. She is now 47 pounds thinner, enjoying her life more, wearing a size 6 instead of a size 10, and says she feels that she is aging gracefully.

SHE LOST 60 POUNDS AND KEPT IT OFF

CATHY BEFORE

CATHY AFTER

Cathy from Iowa was a retired grandmother who spent much of her time working for her church and volunteering. Before she attended one of our seminars and lost 60 pounds, she tried various fad diets with no permanent success.

She did manage to lose 50 pounds with the Weight Watchers program, but gained it all back when she lost interest and stopped going to the meetings. While some might claim that this was a mere lack of self-control, the weight-loss program she was using did nothing to help her develop a new lifestyle. It was simply a program that worked as long as she was attending, but had no lasting effect on her identity, habits or psychological programming.

Like many overweight people in our culture, she saw herself as lazy and unmotivated, and was mad at herself and everyone around her. This self-directed anger turned into depression, which caused her to overeat to feel better. She said there was always an excuse or rationalization for overeating and that's why she kept doing it.

However, Cathy did have a moment of awakening when she had to go on medication for diabetes and high blood pressure. As a result she was the first person to arrive at our weight-loss seminar, which she claimed was her "last ray of hope." She said that she had no other way to go but up. She realized no one else could do it for her; the time had come to take action.

As a result, she lost 60 pounds and completely eliminated her need for high blood pressure medication. Today she only takes her regular daily vitamins. She commented that she "no longer needed to go to the tent maker" to have her clothes made.

Best of all, she began to feel good about her own reflection in the mirror. She no longer saw herself as lazy or unmotivated and went from a person who did not even want to go out the door to a person who had so much energy to burn that she didn't know what to do with it. Not only that, after years of being a "negative person," she changed her programming and became so positive that she joked, "It almost scared her."

Talk about a change of identity.

If you were to talk to Cathy today, she would tell you that the most important thing was remaining consistent and realizing no one else could do it for her. Maintaining a healthy lifestyle is an ongoing process and part of becoming a better person. It's not about the one-time event of losing the weight.

But here is the really interesting thing about the new self-image Cathy developed as a result of losing the weight: her interactions with other people changed completely. When she was overweight, Cathy was a wallflower and in a big hurry to get away from people. Today, her true personality shines in her interactions with others. At last people have a chance to see the real her.

SHE WENT FROM 230 POUNDS TO 137

CAROL BEFORE

CAROL AFTER

In 2003, Carol from Pennsylvania weighed 230 pounds. This was just before attending our weight loss seminar as a result of a personal awakening. During the writing of this book I spoke with her and she is now at a very healthy 137 pounds.

Think about it she has maintained the weight loss for a full six years.

Like many of us, Carol grew up in a household where there was little or no physical activity other than playing outside. As a result, she grew up thinking of exercise as a "pain in the ass," so she didn't feel like doing it. In fact, most of the time she never even thought about it.

Carol tried changing her food habits, taking diet pills, using the Weight Watchers system, skipping meals and counting calories. She lost five or ten pounds here and there, but nothing worked for her consistently and she gained even the smallest amount of weight loss right back. She did not have the willpower to stick with anything she tried.

In fact, Carol claimed she had gone to many classes where she was told what to eat and what not to eat, but none of them actually told her how to make the changes a part of her lifestyle. To add insult to injury, she claimed that knowing certain foods were forbidden made her want them more. This is a prime example of how focusing on what you DON'T want encourages behavior that brings about what you don't want.

What was most interesting was that Carol was in denial about her health. She said she did not think the day would ever come when her weight would be a problem; she thought of herself as healthy, in spite of the fact that she was overweight.

But this all changed when the day she had convinced herself would never come arrived and she was diagnosed with type-two diabetes. That was when she decided to come to our seminar. She had finally realized she was responsible for changing her life. If she had never admitted to this responsibility and embraced it, she would still be heavy today.

Instead, Carol has gone from a size 24 to a size 6. Her entire psychology has changed in regard to her own sense of empowerment, motivation and willpower. Getting up and going to the gymis a regular part of her lifestyle. She actually has the energy and enthusiasm to get up and get going, when before she would have decided to sit in front of the TV and eat.

Carol has also devoted herself to strength training, to maintaining a healthy metabolism and keeping her fat-burning rate high. This is something that can make an enormous difference to long-term success in keeping weight off and remaining healthy. It's also another example of how devotion to constant and never ending improvement is the key to lasting success.

The interesting thing about Carol's journey from being overweight and unhealthy to feeling great about who she is was that she realized how important it was to do it for herself. In fact, she said if you decide to lose weight because someone else tells you to do it, it won't work. This clearly demonstrates the level of self-respect you must have in order to achieve and maintain a healthy lifestyle.

And the people in your life get to enjoy the benefits with you, by having you around healthy, energetic and full of life.

IT'S NOT JUST ABOUT LOSING WEIGHT

As you read these success stories, you may realize that these principles can be used to create other kinds of success in your life. This is probably the most exciting thing you are going to get out of using the material in this book. You are going to develop a new sense of confidence in yourself and a set of principles you can live by, and apply to any area of your life, where you want to make changes for the better.

It all begins with your moment of awakening; the moment when you realize that you are responsible and that you must take action immediately, whether you are ready or not.

For instance, I can remember when I was young and broke and had no future. I took the last $175 I had and spent it on an Anthony Robbins seminar ticket. My friends all thought I was nuts, but I can tell you this: that $175 was probably the wisest investment I ever made.

Anthony Robbins challenged me to believe that there was more to me than I was currently demonstrating. I realized that if I didn't start to take some responsibility for my own life, nothing was going to change.

It was all up to me.

This was a startling realization; and I have had other moments of awakening since then. It caused me to start building momentum and move toward achieving a better life for myself. I won't tell you that it was easy. But that's the name of the game. When it comes to success you take action, succeed and repeat. Or you fail, learn from it, adjust your plan and take action again.

And again. And again. And again.

So how about it?

NOW IT'S YOUR TURN!

Now let me ask you a question: is there any reason whatsoever why you cannot achieve the same kind of success that these people have? To assist you in answering that question, let's take one last look at the common denominators in all of their stories:

Have Your Own Moment of Awakening

First, you will notice that all of them thought everything was pretty much okay until they reached their pivotal moment of awakening. The interesting thing is that despite their awakening, none of them realized how truly dramatic an impact their weight was having on their quality of life. In fact, all of them told me that they did not realize how much more energy and vitality they could have, until they actually experienced the weight loss. One of them had become a complete social wallflower because of it.

So what are you missing out on?

This is the first question to ask yourself to proactively reach your own moment of awakening. Of course, you could always wait until it hits you like a ton of bricks, but I believe you deserve better than that.

Sit down right now and confront denial by making a list of how your weight is affecting your quality of life. I realize you already did this once, but denial is a sneaky little trickster and you'll need to be ruthlessly persistent in order to beat it.

Take Responsibility

No one is going to do this for you. In fact, that's the main reason why I don't even like to take credit for my clients' successes. It's not about me, it's not about my seminars and it's not even about this book you are reading.

This is about you and no one else.

No one will ever care for your body for you nor will they ever be able to. Regardless of how difficult your circumstances might be or how difficult the people around you might be making it for you, you have to decide that you are going to let go of what you can't control and begin taking responsibility for the things you can.

Take a moment right now to write down all the things you can begin doing today to get your body in shape. Then write down all the exterior circumstances or people you have been blaming. Go through the list, one by one, crossing them off.

As you do this, make the commitment to yourself that you're no longer going to blame these people or circumstances, and the respective results, for your own behavior.

Get Rid of Perfectionism

The illusion of perfection is like a mirage in the desert. You can literally chase after it until you are dead and still never catch up with it. The sooner you acknowledge this and stop aiming for perfection, the sooner you will be able to build momentum and motivation, and enjoy the results of positive action. Find the things you have been putting off in regard to achieving your healthy lifestyle and get started on them, whether you are ready or not.

Taking the Next Step

Okay, now that we have the unpleasant stuff out of the way, it's time to get into changing your self-image, developing self-respect and devoting yourself to the consistent pursuit of a healthy lifestyle. These are the principles we will be covering in the remainder of this book.

As we do, it is important to remember that this is not an event. It is a process of constant and never-ending improvement which will become one of the most incredible journeys that you will ever take in your life.

Oscar Wilde once said, “The world belongs to the discontented.” Within this statement is the key that can change your life forever. Over and over and over again. It’ll just keep getting better and better as you look for new ways to improve and to grow.

While you certainly want to make sure that you are happy with who you are, and continue to develop the self-respect required to be

successful, you must always remember to stay on top of the human tendency to become complacent.

Just think of the second law of thermodynamics. Everything is consistently decaying and breaking down....that is unless there is a positive and well-organized energy source constantly flowing into it and through it.

It is a scientific certainty.

This means no matter how much you succeed in life, there is no guarantee you will be able to maintain that level of success without devoting yourself to the consistent cultivation of the habits that brought about that success. This is initially a painful fact of life, but once you accept and embrace it, it becomes one of the greatest pleasures available to you.

It is the opportunity to devote yourself to the process of being the hero of a story big enough to live in and exciting enough to make you a source of inspiration to all those around you.

So how about it?

5

A Preview of

LIFE'S COMING ATTRACTIONS

Have you ever gone to see a movie and been just sucked in by the coming attractions? Amazing marketing job when you think about it…three to five minutes of emotionally charged pictures and sounds and before you know it you're completely sold.

Even if the movie isn't coming out for another month, you say to yourself, "I've got to see that when it comes out!"

Most of the time you don't even think about making the time or finding the money to go see the movie. You simply decide to go see it….even if it isn't going to be out for another month. Why is this? Because movie previews are carefully designed by expert marketers who know all the right emotional buttons to push. Once you become emotionally involved in something, action is inevitable; whether you have all the steps planned out or not.

Such is the power of preview. You know, Albert Einstein said our "Imagination is the preview for life's coming attractions." Why is this? Is it because we can will something to happen simply by thinking about it?

Well, not quite…

However, we can will ourselves to positive action by use of our imagination. All we have to do is know how to create "previews" that will set up a positive emotional vibration in our bodies and move us to action.

On the other hand…we can also will ourselves to inaction by use of our imagination….it's called worry. All we need to do is create a "preview" that will set up a negative vibration in our bodies such as anxiety or fear.

These are the stories that we tell ourselves and since they control our actions, which control our results, they ultimately control our life. Looks like Einstein was pretty spot on about this one. Think about it this is as close to predicting the future that anyone can ever get. So here is the question now, What kinds of previews will help you predict and create the future that you truly desire?

Sure, you might be thinking that you can't predict everything: you can't predict the weather (even the weatherman can't do that all the time and they get paid to do it). You can't control other people and you can't control the immutable laws of nature. However, you can control yourself by aligning your previews with the natural laws that will make your body WANT to be thin. In fact, you can make your body want this bad enough to where you won't even need to know how you are going to accomplish it.

This is the purest and most motivating form of desire. Just think about all of the emergencies in your life that you faced not knowing how you were going to deal with them. However, you were so emotionally involved in them that you found a way anyway. This is precisely the state of mind and body that we are going to create using practical "previewing" techniques.

Before we get started though….let me just say two things:

First: You are not going to become an expert at this overnight. The process of using your imagination to influence your actions is more than just daydreaming. It's an art and a discipline which takes consistent attention and concentrated effort, much like learning a musical instrument. Now is the time to set aside the illusion of perfection and focus instead on direction and progress.

Second: While this is something that you need to practice diligently, it's important that it doesn't become a chore. Have fun with this and if it stops being fun, mix it up. Once you really start to get good get your imagination involved and add your own personal touch to these exercises. When you do, you'll find that it's much easier to get emotionally involved in something that you have helped to create.

And now...

IT'S SHOW TIME!

The first thing that we're going to do is create the picture of your ideal healthy lifestyle. Now, here's something that you'll want to remember as you are doing this: the goal is not to lose weight.

Why?

Well, remember that your affirmations need to be affirmative and the idea of losing anything is hardly good in any case. Think about it you lose your wallet, you lose your job, you lose your hair, you lose your keys just as you are on your way out the door to work, you lose your mind sometimes! These examples represent the way that your subconscious mind interprets loss. Not good.

Now just imagine what impression your subconscious mind gets when you start to talk about losing weight. That said; let's build your previews around what you are going to gain from having a healthier lifestyle.

Okay, so you've decided what your ideal weight is going to be we'll call this your "normal weight." If you are still at a loss on how to determine your ideal weight, there are calculators and tools online that can help you. However, even if you don't have this determined you can still benefit from this exercise.

This is an exercise in strengthening your imaginative capabilities: close your eyes and picture yourself sitting in a movie theatre all alone. It's almost completely black and all that you can really see is the white screen in front of you. Go ahead and do this now. Don't read the next step until you get this image firm in your mind.

Now, when you close your eyes again I want you to engage each one of your senses, one at a time. Notice the smell of the theatre, the feel of the air and of the seat against your back, shoulders and buttocks. You also might notice the feeling of your feet on the floor of the theatre and of your elbows and forearms resting on the arm rests.

You might also become aware of the sounds in the theatre; just let your mind experience whatever occurs to you first. Maybe it's the sound of the film projector starting as the screen goes black, the 20th Century Fox theme playing. Close your eyes and really get into that experience.

Next, comes the fun part. As the screen lights up again, you see yourself and hear pleasant and upbeat music playing. You're walking on the street or on the beach or in the park...wherever you like to walk. Just make sure that it's somewhere you can relate to within the context of your life. Maybe you're alone, or with a friend or a lover or walking your dog.

However, you see that you are at your normal weight. You are wearing the clothes that you would wear if you were at this weight. As you picture this you might notice that you are feeling really excited, secure, sexy or confident. Your facial features, like your cheekbones look more defined because of your weight. Your posture is more upright and confident and your walk more brisk and energetic.

As people pass you and say, "Hello, how are you?" You smile and respond, "Great! Never been better! How about you?" The music swells and you start feeling even better as you are watching yourself. Now take some time to get into this experience and then we'll take the final step.

By now you ought to have a full blown movie preview in front of you... now it's time to step into the role of the "hero" of the movie....that would be you. Next time, as you close your eyes, you begin to float towards the movie screen. Closer and closer you get until you drift right into your own body on the screen.

You are now walking along you may become aware of the feeling of the ground beneath you. Is it the sandy beach under your bare feet? Perhaps the click of your dress shoes as you take a stroll through the mall or on a downtown street? You'll probably become aware of a slight breeze against your skin and of the warm sun on your face and your arms.

Next, move on to the feelings that are in your body…what emotional state are you in? See if you can feel the positive vibration of this emotional state within your body. Breathe in deep as you are walking along, noticing the smell of the air as you do so, and let that feeling expand.

Listen to the sound of the cars rushing by or the birds chirping or the waves against the shore. Now listen closer and pay attention to the other sounds. As you are walking along, pay attention to the way that people are looking at you. Perhaps someone of the opposite sex gives you the once over. Maybe you even see someone who knew you when you were overweight and they are so pleasantly surprised that they ask how you did it.

Close your eyes and spend the next few minutes just taking in this experience and enjoying it. Take your time and make it as real as you possibly can.

Pay close attention to how you feel as you open your eyes again and let me ask you this, If you could feel the way that you do right now how much easier would it be for you to stay committed to the goal of gaining that experience?

Now in case the movie theatre doesn't work for you, there are a few other settings that you can try…

If you are having trouble visualizing yourself, try taking a few pictures of some people who you want to look like. Just be fair to yourself… if you are 5'2" don't pick someone who is 5'11", etc. The idea is to practice superimposing your face onto this person's face. You can even use a scene from a movie if you want.

The purpose of this approach is to provide you with some "training wheels" to get you going. As soon as you get to where you can conjure up the image in your mind without looking at the picture, get rid of it and simply work on using your imagination alone.

Again, do this until you can actually feel the emotional vibration in your body. Take a "snapshot" of that feeling and as you do, speak one of your affirmations out loud. This will create an anchor point between that emotion and the affirmation; and will compel you to action even faster.

Put this into consistent practice, make it a daily habit and just see where it gets you in one year. I'm guessing you'll be blown away by the results.

Now let's talk about stepping this up a notch…

SYNTHESIZING YOUR EXPERIENCE

If you have ever been in a play (even if it was as far back as grade school) you probably remember that they had something called "dress rehearsals." This is where you get into costume and act out the entire play as if it were the final performance. If this is how people prepare for a play, which is make believe, it would probably be a good idea to do the same thing in preparing yourself for your new lifestyle.

This means creating a synthetic experience of your ideal lifestyle or behavior. Let's say there is a car that you really want to buy and you can do one of two things: You can sit and imagine yourself in it, put pictures of it up on your refrigerator or….

…you can go down to the car lot, sit in it and test drive it. Which one do you think is going to compel you to action faster? If you doubt this, just ask any car salesman how much easier it is to make a sale if they send the person home in the car for one night.

By the same standard, creating a synthetic experience of what your dream lifestyle looks like can compel you to take the action which will bring about the results that lead to that lifestyle. You might have heard of Jack Canfield, the best selling co-author of the "Chicken Soup for the Soul" series...

Jack Canfield often talks about how he used to go to "come as you will be" parties where every guest would dress up and act like the person that they wanted to be in the future. Aspiring international consultants came with business cards and when they spoke with other party guests they spoke about their international consulting business as if it were a reality.

As silly as this may sound, it plays an amazing trick on your emotions and your subconscious mind....it builds belief in something which has not happened yet. So much belief to where the mind and body responds with plans and ideas that seem to come from out of nowhere and with consistent motivation to act on those plans.

The people who attend these parties often end up where they want to be or, at least, pretty close. This is the influence that a synthesized experience can have in your life; the trick is to learn how to create them.

Now, creating a synthetic experience of yourself at normal weight may not be as easy as attending a "come as you will be" party. However, there are some things that you can begin to do today which will help you quite a bit in creating the previews for your life's coming attractions:

Synthesize your desired behaviors

If you are having trouble with leaving food on your plate, practice actually doing it several times a day. This doesn't mean that you have to eat several times a day; it just means that you give your subconscious more chances to build the synthesized experience of saying no to clearing your plate. Here is how...

At the end of your meal, make sure that you leave a few bites of food on your plate and literally push it away from you with the food on it. As you do, you want to associate that action with a positive emotion. This will condition you to associate saying no to food with pleasure. In time, this will begin to override the conditioning that clearing your plate is the desired course of action.

For example, as you push your plate away smile as big as you can and say: "Ah! Now that feels good!" You can even lean back and stretch, clap your hands once, crank up your favorite music, start dancing or singing. You can even say one of your affirmations. Do whatever it takes to create a strong feeling of happiness and pleasure in your body.

Again, this will give your subconscious a positive emotion to anchor to the behavior which will help you to lose weight. Now, here is the trick: do this several times at the end of one meal, putting your plate back in front of you and picking up your fork again before pushing the food away (just no cheating and taking a bite while you are at it!).

This might be kind of hard, but the more you anchor this behavior to a positive emotion the easier it will become. In fact, don't be surprised if you notice a difference after one or two meals. In addition to reconditioning your mind to associate pleasure with saying no to food, this will also keep you from overeating.

Here is why:

It takes twenty minutes for the message to get from your stomach to your mind that you have had enough to eat. Think about it, how many times have you eaten a second helping thinking that it was okay and then ended up with a stomach ache? Pushing your plate away several times like this and associating this action with a pleasurable emotion will give your body some time to assess whether it has had enough or not.

Think about it when you overeat it is almost never because you are still hungry. It's because you are craving more food because it gives you pleasure. So what do most people do when they are trying not to overeat? They try to push the plate away by sheer force of will, grimacing in pain as they do.

The problem with this is that the mind associates eating with pleasure and further associates saying no to food with pain or punishment. So, on one side you have overeating and experience pleasure and on the other you have pushing the food away and experiencing feelings of being in pain, punished or restricted.

I'll give you three guesses which path will be easier to take....and the first two don't count.

However, if you take the time to create a synthetic experience of pleasure and your mind begins to associate that pleasure with saying no to food while it is still on your plate....

....you get the idea.

This same pattern can be used to condition yourself to associate positive emotions with any of the following behaviors:

- Getting up and putting on your gym clothes to exercise

  Every time that you do this, visualize your fat cells falling off as you are jogging or walking on the stair master. Visualize people walking by and checking out your new body.

- Saying no when someone offers you food

  Saying no when you are offered food is often associated with feelings of guilt, like you "let the person down." Instead of making yourself responsible for another person's feelings of rejection and disappointment (which most of the time are only in your head) celebrate your own decision to do something which is going to make YOU happy.

  If the other person wants to harp on you about it, tell them what you are doing and how excited you are about it. If they don't support you, then their opinion is self-serving and not worth your attention anyway.

- Not eating when you get a craving

  A craving is an indication of an emotional need, not a physical one. Most of the time when we get a craving we start thinking: what do I want to eat? Next time you get a craving, visualize that feeling as being a strong desire to be at your normal weight instead of a desire to eat.

  While your conditioning will fight you on this, you will come out ahead if you are consistent and persistent; and if you master the use of your creative imagination.

  And finally…

- Whenever you lose a pound

  Too often we don't celebrate the small victories in our life. We wait to have the big celebration once we've lost 30, 40 or 80 lbs. Meanwhile if we mess up even ONCE along the way we're ready to give ourselves a paper cut and pour lemon juice and hot sauce all over it.

Instead of this approach, treat each little victory as an opportunity to recondition yourself to associate pleasure with getting closer to your normal weight. You can do this by visualizing yourself in front of a live audience who is giving you a standing ovation.

Again, work on creating whatever synthetic experience you need in order to recondition your body so that it wants to be thin. These exercises will help you move toward what you want faster with more energy and enthusiasm…

…but we aren't done just yet…

A ROACH ON A BIRTHDAY CAKE: THE POWER OF NEGATIVE

Anchors

Sorry if you have a birthday coming up, but just think about what happened when you read the above statement. I can tell you one thing, I remember in home economics class in high school when they passed out a "fun facts" worksheet about what is in some of the foods that we eat (and I'm not talking about fats, sugars, sodium, pesticide or preservatives either).

Sparing the details of these "fun facts," I can remember that there were certain foods that many of my friends and classmates said that they would never eat again. Now, there is a very important lesson to be learned from this:

If you can condition yourself to associate positive emotions with a certain behavior or experience, you can also condition yourself to associate negative emotions with it. This kind of conditioning is accomplished by the use of negative anchors and it can provide you with additional motivation to rid yourself of the behaviors which can keep you from achieving your normal weight.

For example, when you picture a roach on a birthday cake you probably feel a little grossed out don't you? I bet if we really went into detail about it, I could get you to stop eating cake….at least for a while.

This is because I created an image in your mind that got you to associate a negative anchor with birthday cake….a cockroach. So, how can you begin to use the process of negative anchoring to your advantage? Let's take a few examples...

Before you proceed I'm going to warn you....this may be difficult if you have a weak stomach. If you feel that you may not be ready for this, go ahead and skip to the next chapter....

Still with me? Okay, here we go...

Let's assume that you are having trouble with being tempted to a certain kind of ice cream....I mean you get up in the middle of the night and eat three or four spoonfuls of it just because you have a craving for it. This can really keep you from reaching your normal weight and can be a blow to your self-confidence if you continue to give in to it.

But what if you were to create a negative anchor to the idea of eating this ice cream? For instance, picture yourself eating a mouthful of it and suddenly biting into something crunchy. As you spit it out, you find that you just bit into a one and a half inch long cockroach.

You also notice that a few of its legs are missing, which means that you may have accidently eaten them without realizing it. Not only that, the crunch broke its exoskeleton and that stuff that looks like mayonnaise came out.

Ugh!

How about if you are tempted to drink something that is high in sugar which your body easily stores as fat? You are drinking it out of a can, so you don't notice at first but....when you get to the bottom you find that there is a large hairball at the bottom of it.

Feeling sick yet? Okay, just one more...

Let's say that you're addicted to a certain kind of candy which uses gelatin in it. However, one day you find out that this candy is actually made using the hooves of cows. Can you guess what those cows are stepping in all day?

Now unlike the first two examples, this one is actually true. Do a little research on how gelatin is made and you may just find that you have no problem saying no to anything that contains it. Again, this is the power that a negative anchor can have in changing your conditioning about certain foods.

It's like those old jokes where you ask, "What's grosser than gross?" When the other person says, "I don't know," you follow up with something absolutely repulsive like, "You get done eating a bowl of white rice only to watch the last one crawl away." Or "You're eating a bowl of flakey cereal and find out that your brother is missing his scab collection."

Okay, you ready to take a lunch break?

How about a snack....maybe some ice cream?

Now, I realize that this might seem kind of extreme and maybe even a bit offensive. However, remember that being overweight is putting you at a greater risk for heart disease, diabetes and it is having a poor effect on the quality of your life.

Yes, I may be grossing you out right now, but I believe that you deserve better than what you were giving yourself before you picked up with book and I'm determined to see you achieve it.

So the next time that you get a temptation to eat something that you KNOW isn't going to be good for you, use one of these negative anchors. Literally stop yourself and create the most disgusting synthetic experience that you can imagine. Make this a habit and see how much easier it is for you to turn away from temptation.

So now you have a pretty good toolbox of previews to help you create the coming attractions of your life. But you may also be aware that simply creating previews is not all that there is to being successful with your health. There are things to take into account which are beyond your control and they can work for or against you.

What I am talking about is the self-evident and immutable laws which govern all of creation. When it comes to these laws you have only two choices:

Seek to understand them and to adjust your actions according to what you really want.

Or...

Whether by ignorance or stubbornness, you can try to “break” them and find that you can only break yourself against them.

I’m guessing one of those choices sounds better than the other, so let’s have a look at these laws…

6

Becoming a Natural,

LAW ABIDING CITIZEN

If you have never had that phrase said to you, you're doing well. However, right now you may be in violation of laws that are much more unforgiving than the laws of the land. These are the laws of nature. They are in control of the circumstances of your life, whether you

like them, believe them, accept them or even understand them.

You might have heard this one before; "Ignorance of the law is no excuse for breaking the law." Now, while I'm not here to point any fingers, there is something very important to learn from this statement in regard to the natural laws of the universe: ignorance does not spare you the natural consequences of these laws.

However, you can gain an understanding of them and actually use them to your advantage to achieve your normal weight. In fact, the more you understand about these laws, the more you can use them to get what you want in any area of your life.

We are going to cover six basic laws:

1. The Law Of Attraction
2. The Law Of Polarity
3. The Law Of Rhythm
4. The Law Of Relativity
5. The Law Of Cause And Effect
6. The Law Of Energy

Let's start with the Law of Attraction...

NATURE'S MATCH-MAKING SYSTEM: THE LAW OF ATTRACTION

Most of the time when we think of attraction we think about being attracted to a potential mate. However, there is actually evidence of the law of attraction all over nature. For example, when you place a seed in the ground it actually begins to draw in the nutrients from its surroundings and to transform them into a plant.

You may be wondering what this has to do with achieving your ideal weight... the answer is that human beings also tend to be attracted to things which are consistent with what is inside them. In other words, your beliefs and perceptions determine the dominating thoughts in your mind, which in turn determine the things you are most attracted to.

When I say attracted, it's important to realize that this attraction is not always positive. For example, if you are constantly thinking about how badly you want to eat a piece of fried chicken, you are more likely to notice the sign for a KFC. On a deeper level, if you believe that the world is a dangerous place and people can't be trusted, you'll be quick to recognize (or even imagine) anything that validates that belief.

You see, being attracted to something simply means that you are more aware of it and that you are drawn toward it in some way. At the same time, your Reticular Activation System will work to filter out anything that is not relevant to the dominating thoughts in your mind.

For example, close your eyes and picture the word "you" for several seconds....

Okay, now keep the image of the word "you" in your mind. Go to the top of this page and scan it quickly looking for every occurrence of the word "if."

Not easy, right?

Now go back and with the word "you" in your mind and look for every occurrence you can find of the word "you." As you may notice, it's a lot easier to recognize the word that is dominating your conscious mind. This is one example of the law of attraction at work and it is a demonstration of why it's so important for you to create synthetic experiences of what you WANT, instead of what you don't want. By focusing on what you do want, you can be assured that your actions will be aligned with what you want.

However, if you are always thinking about what you don't want you are going to be drawn to what you don't want; and that is the thing that will influence your actions. If you are looking for solid evidence of this, all you have to do is look at the way violent criminals develop their habits.

Sociologists tell us that when people are first introduced to crime they are turned off by it. However, after enough exposure they begin to become comfortable with it and pretty soon they begin to tolerate it. After enough time and exposure, it begins to dominate their thoughts (both conscious and unconscious), and they finally become influenced by it.

This is the very thing that causes a person to go to prison for several decades, and only to end up back in again after being released. People move toward things that are the most familiar, whether those things are beneficial to them or not. And what is most familiar to us?

The thoughts, ideas, feelings and images that dominate our minds and influence the emotional states of our bodies. Think about it some people continue to get into the same kinds of relationships where they get hurt….really hurt. However, they keep dating the same kinds of people because that is what is familiar to them. The same can be true with your eating habits, financial decisions or anything else in your life.

Such is the power of the law of attraction. That is why it's so important to get your "inner game" mastered if you want to have a healthy lifestyle. You do this by focusing on what you want instead of what you don't want, and doing it consistently, so that it becomes the dominating obsession of your mind and body.

However, there is another reason why it is important to get on the right side of the law of attraction by focusing on what you really want: if you do not engage the law of attraction on purpose by choosing your thoughts, someone else will choose them for you. I know, it sounds like some weird conspiracy theory you'd read in a science fiction book, but allow me to clarify.

Go ahead and clear your mind of as much inner dialogue as you can. Forget about really paying attention and just kind of tune out; don't think about anything in particular.

Now scan this paragraph quickly and tell me what you see:

"Your mind cannot ***NOTICE*** *every single detail that it is exposed to on a day to day basis. Therefore,* ***THAT*** *little thing called the reticular activation system is at work filtering out* ***YOUR*** *experiences according to what your mind considers relevant. Right now your* ***MIND*** *is not engaged in directing this filtering and so what you are seeing here* ***IS*** *the most obvious by default. Therefore, I can use this opportunity to get* ***MY*** *message to you without you having a chance to determine whether I am trying to* ***PREY*** *on you and get you to believe something that is not true."*

Now you might be thinking, of course my mind is not this person's prey. However, your subconscious doesn't know that.…it just accepts the most dominating ideas it is fed and these ideas eventually form your conditioning.

You may not think you have anything to worry about because no one is "out to get you." However, remember that every day you are exposed to messages created with the intention of soliciting some kind of action from you. It's called advertising and the food industry spends billions on it every year.

If you consider the popular foods that are being promoted, it's not hard to see why so many people in our society are overweight.
Most people spend a number of their waking hours worrying about something they are afraid will happen or they simply going on autopilot. As a result, they are attracted to things which are influencing them to get more of what they don't want or they are attracted to what someone else has manipulated them to be attracted to. This default allows someone else to influence their thinking.

Does this mean that you need to live in a cave, get rid of your television and wear blinders every time you go to the store?

No. But it does mean that if you want to choose your own future according to what YOU want, then you have to get on the right side of the law of attraction. Here is how:

- Decide what you WANT
- Make it the dominating obsession of your thoughts by using affirmations and synthetic experiences

This will change your beliefs and your perceptions. It will change what you are attracted to and it will change your life. You'll also notice that something will happen that I'm not sure I completely understand myself:

Odd little things that seem like coincidences will begin to occur. These things will be consistent with the new ideas you are focusing on. You might be at the store and find that the person in line next to you is a personal trainer. While you are speaking to them, they mention a specific type of workout that is getting great results for their clients.

The next day when you walk into work, one of your coworkers might have that book on their desk and you ask them about it. They tell you that it's working well for them and you should check it out. You don't mention it to anyone, but about a week later a friend of yours lends you the book because they think you might find it interesting.

This is just an example…and I could spend several pages explaining the reasoning behind this side of the law of attraction. However, I'm not sure that anyone can fully explain why it works this way. The point is it happens, and once you begin to deliberately choose your thoughts and emotional states using the affirmations and synthetic experiences, you'll see what I mean.

The point is not whether you fully understand the law of attraction. The information and evidence you have seen in the examples I have given ought to be enough for you to decide what action to take.

Like everything else in life, the law of attraction can be used either for good or for ill.

Speaking of….

NATURE'S DOUBLE EDGED SWORD: THE LAW OF POLARITY

When you see half a glass of water, do you see it as half empty or half full?

It's a little old, I know. However, it illustrates one of the fundamental laws of creation: the law of polarity. The law of polarity states that everything has two sides and that each is necessary to define the other. In other words, there is no up if it cannot be compared to a down; there is no dark if there is no light (because there is no way to determine what dark even is); without the outside, there is no inside.

There is no positive thought if it cannot be contrasted with a negative thought. The law of polarity provides the context through which we can define two opposing sides of something. There is no way around this if you take away one, it completely changes the other because the context changes.

The key to success in building your healthy lifestyle is taking the law of polarity into account in everything you do. And in case you think I'm just going to tell you to be positive, think again.

Positive and negative aren't what matters; what matters is what is going to support your goal and what is not. Let me give you an example: cheesecake tastes great to most of us, even if we eat seven pieces of it. Sure, we may get burned out if we do this every day for a week. However, the "positive" side of eating cheesecake is pretty nice. However, there is another side to this: it's the fact that too much cheesecake makes your clothes shrink after a while.

Then you have to buy new ones...bummer.

So we have a positive side and a negative side....sort of. You see, when someone decides to eat too much cheesecake they're not being negative; they're doing it because there is a positive benefit, because that's what they are focused on.

However, let's take a look at the opposite decision....deciding to refrain from eating cheesecake when you get the urge. Well, that also has a "positive" and a "negative" side: the positive side is being thinner and healthier while the negative side is that you miss out on something that gives you pleasure.

Now, if it's all about being positive, you could go one way or the other....you could overindulge for the positive benefit of tasting something great or...

....you could choose the positive benefit of being healthy. Now, someone watching could say that the decision to overeat is negative, because it can lead to ill health. Another person might claim that the cake tastes great and you should go for it.

So who is right?

Well, you could argue that point all day long. The law of polarity always guarantees that you'll have a "positive" side to take. However, the real question is this:

"In what way can I use this circumstance or opportunity to strengthen my commitment to my goal?"

This is the only way to find the true "positive" in any situation and to make sure that NOTHING distracts you from getting what you are after. Let me give you a few examples:

Let's say you come to work one day and your boss has brought donuts for everyone for breakfast. You already had a nice healthy breakfast and you're feeling great, but those donuts sure look good; and they even have your all-time-favorite flavor.

Now, you have a choice to make. You can either say, "Oh my God! I'm trying to lose weight and I'm being tempted by these delicious donuts...and I CAN'T HAVE ONE!"

(A little violin music, please...) But is there a yin to this yang?

Of course. Let's look at the question again:

"In what way can I use this circumstance or opportunity to strengthen my commitment to my goal?"

Now, if you're really stuck in a disempowering pattern of thought you might say:

"There is no way this can help me! It's just a dirty temptation!"

Oh, woe is me....or....

How about practicing your negative anchors? (Just don't announce them out loud.) Perhaps you can remember that you are what you eat and picture all of your coworkers with donut heads.

Might be good for a laugh.

Or you could picture your co-workers coming to you six months from now with the inevitable comment, *"Wow, you look so good! How did you do it?"*

Ah, victory! Now that tastes better than a donut any day!

How about when it's time to go to the gym and exercise? You could say, *"Ugh, time to go to the gym. I'm so tired and I hate the stair master."*

I'm still looking, but I've yet to find someone who actually enjoys the stair master. Sure, some might claim to, but I bet if there were another way to get the same results they'd abandon it in a heartbeat. So why do they do it? Because they enjoy punishment or because they are more focused than the average person?

They do it because they love the results they get from using the stair master. That's what they're thinking about, and sometimes, that's the only thing that keeps them committed every day just ask one of them. If you can tell me another reason, I'd love to hear it.

By now, you are probably beginning to see a relationship between the law of polarity and the law of attraction. The key to benefiting from them is not using them to get what you want. It's getting on the right side of them by properly aligning your thoughts and actions with what you want, not what you don't want.

Again, the question is this:

"In what way can I use this circumstance or opportunity to strengthen my commitment to my goal?"

Hold that thought and let's keep moving...

NATURE'S PACESETTER: THE LAW OF RHYTHM

If there is a law that people have the most difficult time understanding, it's this one. Have you ever seen those diets that say you can lose 30 pounds in 30 days? You may have even tried this kind of diet or at least been tempted to.....who wouldn't?

On the surface it sounds like a pretty good deal and considering how advanced we have become as a race, it might even seem reasonable. After all, we now have super computers that can execute three trillion floating point computations per second!

So it would make sense that we could apply advanced medical science and work out a way for you to lose 30 pounds in 30 days, right? Well, if that's the line of thinking, I've got a better idea.

Amputation.

I think something good to start with might be a foot, because then you could get into a wheelchair and park in the handicapped space. You might even be able to get fitted with a super light weight prosthetic and take your whole leg up to the thigh.

Now, this may sound a little ridiculous, but it IS a solution for losing weight just like the 30 day diet. The reason most of use wouldn't even consider the amputation diet is what we could actually be losing. However, in the 30 day diet, the body is being forced to lose water and tissues, which are important to keeping you in good health.

This is not going to change, no matter what kind of diet you go on. This is because the body has a natural pace and process by which it loses AND gains weight. This is a natural law and no amount of technology can undermine a natural law.

Instead, you have to learn how to get on the right side of this law. This is the law of rhythm, which states that there are seasons in life and there is a pace by which natural systems (such as your body) grow, develop and change.

Lack of alignment with the law of rhythm is one of the leading causes for failure in just about anything. For example, when someone learns a new musical instrument, they expect to pick it up right away. However, the coordination and knowledge required to play a musical instrument simply will not develop overnight.....or even in a few weeks for that matter.

Again, this is because the human body, (of which the mind is a part), is a natural system that develops according to its own pace and rhythms. For some people, this pace is quicker, and the ebb and flow of development is much more evenly spaced. For others the pace is slower, and the ups and downs of the developmental process are a little harder to predict.

The bottom line is in order to successfully develop your mind and body for the weight loss we have been talking about in this book, you are going to have to respect the law of rhythm, and focus more on direction and progress, than on instant results or perfection.

Your body is not a machine, it's an organic life form; and you have to respect that if you want to win at achieving your normal weight. If you treat it like a machine and expect results to come at anything more than a natural pace or if you don't accept that there will be times when your results come faster and easier than others, you are going to end up overwhelmed by disappointment.

Approach the reconditioning of your mind and body the way a farmer would approach the cultivation of land and the growing of crops: you do everything you can, according to the natural principles you are learning in this book, and nature will do its part according to its own rhythm and pace.

Expecting anything different is inviting disappointment and possibly even depression. To assist you in this, here is an affirmation you can use:

"I acknowledge that my body is a natural system and that as long as I do my part in reconditioning my mind and living a healthy lifestyle, my body will respond accordingly."

Of course you also want to use the affirmation for your specific goal weight. Respect the pace at which nature responds to your efforts and enjoy the journey you'll be glad you did.

In case this sounds too easy, let's look at another law that can help you align yourself with the law of rhythm….

Nature's Illusionist: The Law of Relativity

Let's do a little exercise. Pick something in the room that is the size of your own body or bigger.

Got it? Good.

Now walk up to it, look at it close up and hold your hand right up to it. What is bigger, your hand or the object? Pretty simple and straightforward, right?

Turn around and walk about fifteen steps, then hold your hand up and compare it to the object again. Of course you know which one is actually bigger. However, from where you are standing now, your hand probably appears to be about the same size, doesn't it?

You know better than this, but bear with me for just a moment and think about this: your perception of the difference between the two depends on where you are standing. In other words, it's relative.

When you think about it, there is only one thing that causes you to realize they are the same size: your understanding of the law of relativity. You know your position relative to each object is distorting your perception, so you're able to discern their true difference in size.

But what does this have to do with your success at achieving a healthy lifestyle? Simple; it's a reminder that you can't always trust your physical senses to tell you the truth. Instead, you must use your understanding of the law of relativity to assess your situation.

For example, have you ever known someone who has lost or gained a lot of weight? Chances are if you hadn't seen them in a long time, it seemed that there was a BIG difference. However, that is because you had only two images to compare: the thin image and the not-so-thin-image.

However, the person whose weight was changing was able to compare the image they saw in the mirror every morning and every evening, and perhaps, even at times in between. Consequently, they only saw small, subtle changes. Either their subconscious mind dismissed these changes, or they were so minute their Reticular Activation System filtered them out as being irrelevant.

Of course, if they were weighing themselves everyday they would notice a difference. They would also notice whether their clothes were getting tighter or looser.

But if they were to rely only on their own sense and perceptions without having some objective way to measure the changes, they might not have noticed them at all. You would notice them because you saw the situation from a different perspective.

You see, perspective matters....a lot. It determines your perception of things and it can actually fool your physical senses. The only way to overcome this is to use your inner eye, understanding the law of relativity in order to keep track of what is really happening in your life.

That's why the inner game of weight loss is just as important (if not more important), than the outer game. The bottom line is you cannot trust your senses to tell you the truth. Therefore, you look in the mirror and think, "This is not working! I'm still fat and I still don't like the way I look." Don't get discouraged or give up. If you do, you're letting your senses have the final say, in spite of the fact that they are so easily fooled.

Instead, you are going to need some way to measure your progress that is not open to false perception. That is the reason so many people weigh themselves and keep track of their progress from week to week. However, remember that simply losing weight is not an indication that you are building a healthy lifestyle. You also need to make sure you are losing the right kind of weight and changing the mental and emotional conditioning that has made you overweight.

Some additional tools you can use to objectively measure your progress are:

- A Fat Caliper

  This way you can measure your fat percentage and make sure you are losing the right kind of weight. Just be sure you are writing down your measurements on a weekly or daily basis. This will give you a point of reference for tracking your results, and something you can use as a reminder when you get discouraged.

- A Camera

By far the most effective tool for measuring progress, and one which will give you something amazing to show your friends and family members, is a series of weekly pictures. Think about it why do you want to achieve your ideal weight in the first place? You want to look great and to feel great, of course!

Taking pictures is the best way to verify that you are making the desired changes in your physical appearance. Just remember your inner image of yourself is and always will be the most important factor in achieving your normal weight.

- Measuring your Resting Heart Rate

Since your objective is to look and to feel great, you need to be measuring what kind of impact your new lifestyle is having on your overall health and energy level. The concrete way to measure this is by measuring your resting heart rate. As your heart becomes stronger and healthier and your weight more normal your resting heart rate will slow down.

It will take some time, but if you write down your progress and use the other measuring tools, you will find that the overall condition of your body is improving as you get closer to your normal weight.

- A Scale

Again, make sure you are keeping track of your progress; and most importantly use the scale *in conjunction with the other measuring tools!* This will help you focus more on having a healthy body and lifestyle and less on weight loss.

Using these measuring tools will keep you from relying just on your senses, which as you can see will not always tell you the truth.

And speaking of telling the truth…

NATURE'S FEEDBACK SYSTEM: THE LAW OF CAUSE AND EFFECT

You might have heard this before: numbers don't lie, people do. If not, just think about the basic concept of the law of relativity. If you can't always trust your senses to tell you the truth, you have to find another way to measure the circumstances and events around you.

If you don't do this, it will be almost impossible to be honest and objective with yourself and others. Thankfully, there is a natural law that gives you all the feedback you need to learn how to use the principles of nature to your advantage.

The Law of Cause and Effect

In other words, causes and effects are interconnected. For each circumstance or outcome, there is a connected cause. On the other hand, every action or event is a cause set in motion which will inevitably bring about some kind of effect.

Now, I know you might be thinking this is too obvious to mention. However, the Law of Cause and Effect is often overlooked, and overlooking it can keep you from learning the natural principles that control your results.

In case your head is spinning from that last statement, let's take a real world example. Several years ago there was a series of lawsuits filed against fast food restaurants by individuals who blamed the establishments for "making them fat." Shortly after that, there was a law passed called the "common sense law," which stated that people ought to have sense enough to be responsible for their own eating habits.

The "common sense law" pretty much refers to the law of cause and effect in the same way that judges do when it comes to manmade laws:

"Ignorance of the law is no excuse."

And why is it no excuse in regard to the law of cause and effect? Because all it takes is asking yourself these two questions whenever you do anything:

"What is the potential outcome of this action?"

And then…

"Am I going to be pleased with the outcome?"

At the same time, you can ask yourself these three questions when observing the current circumstances and conditions of your life?

"What specific actions and events are responsible for this circumstance or" condition?"

And then…

"What is my share of responsibility in initiating these actions or events?"

And finally…

"In what way can I adjust my future actions to get more of what I want and less of what I don't want?"

In other words, take responsibility for what you have control of, change what you need to change, and let the rest go.

Done deal.

Again, this may seem too obvious to state, but often we take our eyes off the ball when it comes to looking at the events and circumstances of our lives. We get so caught up in the immediate effects of our actions that we aren't able to step back and consider the bigger picture.

I suspect this is the reason many people feel that their life is out of control and that they are victims of circumstance instead of the creators of circumstance.

When we lose sight of the bigger picture, it becomes harder for us to make the connection between our present circumstances and our past actions, as well as our present actions and future circumstances. This victim mentality makes it far too easy to blame other people and events that are out of our control, instead of acknowledging that we are in control.

However, proper observation of the Law of Cause and Effect has a liberating quality that can put you back in control of your life. As the Nazarene said:

"Then you will know the truth and the truth will set you free."

He just forgot to mention that before it sets you free it might make you a little mad.....maybe even at yourself. This is okay as long as the anger is immediately redirected into positive plans of action.

The Law of Cause and Effect will provide you with the bare bones truth about how to create that plan of action and get busy.

This is where the final law, and by far the most powerful law, of nature comes to your aid...

NATURE'S RECYCLING SYSTEM: THE LAW OF ENERGY

Ever get the feeling that you don't have any energy at the end of the day?

If so, it might surprise you to know that it is actually impossible to run out of energy.

Why is this?

Because all you are is energy!

Everything you can see, feel, taste, smell, touch and even what you cannot is energy in some form or another. You've probably heard of Albert Einstein's $E=MC^2$ equation...but what does it mean?

It means that energy (E) is the same thing as matter (M) times the speed of light squared (C^2). Now I'm not a physicist, but I know enough to know that this is telling us something very interesting about matter...

Matter is simply a form of energy at a very high rate of vibration. Everything in the entire universe is composed of energy: your hand, the roof over your head, the clothes you are wearing, and even this book.

It's all energy.

Now, don't tell me you don't have any energy!

Well then, you may be wondering what happens when you don't have the energy to do something. Well, think of it this way it happens the same way you "run out" of money. It doesn't actually go anywhere it simply changes from being in your possession to being in someone else's.

The same is true with energy. Energy can never be destroyed....it can only change form. For example, when you take your trash out, it goes to the dumpster and then to the trash truck. Eventually it makes it to the landfill and most of it is going to get burned. However, as it actually turns into smoke particles and floats into the air, some of it becomes ash. It's never destroyed....it simply changes form.

The same thing with all of your energy; it never goes away, it simply changes direction. For example, if you had to carry a 50 pound weight around with you all day, you'd notice that you have "less" energy. However, in reality that energy is being used to support the additional effort to carry the weight around.

Now think about this if you are overweight, your energy is being used to carry that extra weight and to feed and support the additional cells. Your heart has to work harder, so more energy is directed toward the survival of your organism. This means you have less energy to spend in additional activities like running, walking, riding a bike, playing with your kids when you get home

from work, thinking (yes, that takes physical energy), and....brace yourself...sex.

It's not that you don't have less energy for these activities it's that the energy is being directed toward other things. In other words, that energy is *feeding* that spare tire, and working to keep it alive.

Let's take a closer look. What do you think happens to something when more energy is being directed at it? Well it grows, of course, unless it's the type of energy that an atomic bomb gives off.

However, in most cases, when it comes to your body, energy is used to feed and to nourish. Remember, your body is simply another form of energy and in order for it to survive it needs to be consistently fed energy. This is because your body is constantly replacing its cells to keep you healthy and to rid your body of things that could cause sickness and disease.

In fact, within seven years the body that you are sitting in right now will be made of a completely new material. Same blueprint, but the materials will have been completely replaced.

Do you know what this means? This means that you really ARE what you eat. You've probably heard this before, but think about it right now....if your body is constantly rebuilding itself, what is it using to do so?

Energy.

And where does it get that energy from? From the food you eat, which is broken down and converted into a different form of energy, in order to build the body you are now living in. If this isn't enough to inspire you to change your eating habits, let's take a closer look and tie all of these natural laws together...

Everything starts out as energy and the direction in which that energy is directed determines what the energy is used to create or nourish. Let's pretend you start thinking about how overeating is making you overweight.

As your energy and attention is focused on this, it invokes the law of attraction, which determines your perception of the things around you, as well as what you are drawn to and what is drawn to you. As you are drawn to something it creates a greater presence in your consciousness and your Reticular Activation System begins to filter and shape your experience accordingly.

You see yourself as overweight and everything you experience is a reflection of what you are focusing your energy on. You think about how it is overeating that's making you that way...You think about how horrible you feel because people look at you as "fat" and that affects your impression of how other people look at you and treat you.

While your energy is focused on these things, the law of polarity is invoked because there is less energy for focusing on other things in your life. You are less focused on renewing your conditioning, and eating healthy, and less focused on how you want to be thin and how good it is going to feel.

When energy is focused like this, your actions, thoughts and habits naturally follow the same path; and the law of cause and effect is invoked. The more you think about being overweight and overeating (whether you are trying to stop or not), the more your actions align themselves with such things.

You're more tempted by junk food and as you feel worse and worse about your body, you put less energy into taking care of it. The law of cause and effect reciprocates by bringing you more of what your energy is focused on. Meanwhile, you have less energy to use in order to create what you really want.

This cycle continues and as it creates more of what you are focused on. The law of relativity causes everything else to become small in comparison, including the way out of this self-defeating cycle. The more you think about being overweight, the more these natural laws cause energy to be directed toward building and creating more of what you are focusing on.

Thought energy creates perceptions and sets up a vibration in your body which is consistent with those thoughts. This vibration influences your emotional state and converts that thought energy into action.... and as that energy continues to feed and support those thoughts, they become a solid reality.

$E=MC^2$

Now think about this one again, "You are what you eat." Do you think this is simply talking about food?

Think about it your physical body is nothing more or less than energy. Just as food is made of energy, and just as the thoughts that set up the physical vibrations you interpret as emotions are a form of energy. This is a scientific fact which is supported by these irrefutable laws of nature.

Changing the state of your physical body is going to require changing the type of energy that you are using in order to create it: this means the thoughts you are allowing yourself to become emotionally involved in, as well as the foods you are allowing into your stomach.

All you need to do is decide what kind of body you want to create, focus on what you really want and align your perceptions and beliefs. This will create a stronger attraction between you and the things which will help you to get what you want. (The Law of Attraction)

As this attraction grows, you'll become even more aware of what is going to help you reach your goal and less aware of what is going to keep you from reaching it. (The Law of Polarity).

As this continues, your actions will be further influenced and supported by the things which dominate your experience. These actions will cause you to direct your energy toward getting the results that you want. (The Law of Cause and Effect).

As your thoughts, emotional state and actions continue to shape your experience and perception, the obstacles will become like anthills next to the image of your goal. (The Law of Relativity).

Add a little patience and acknowledge that your body is an organic system and not a machine, and that in time these laws will bring about the desired results. (The Law of Rhythm).

In time, the energy you have directed toward getting what you want (E) will become the very thing you have desired (M), according to the intensity of your effort to achieve it (C^2).

That's how the Law of Energy can be leveraged to get what you want…

Now let's put this plan into action, shall we?

7

Foods, Moods

AND ATTITUDES

You might be wondering if we're going to get into meal plans, exercising routines, and calorie counting now.

Hardly.

There is already plenty of free information available about developing a healthy lifestyle with proper diet and exercise. In fact, most of us know all about that the problem is we aren't using what we know.

And why is that?

It's all about your conditioning. What we are going to do is develop a plan for adopting healthy eating habits. This requires harnessing the energy that drives all your decisions and actions.

That energy is your emotions.

Most of the time we like to think we're driven by reasoning factors. However, this is greatly underestimating the role of our emotions. It is also giving our reasoning factors far more responsibility than they can handle.

You see examples of this all the time when people don't take their own advice. They think because they have a logical understanding of something they "should" be able to put it into practice. However, people only act on things that have either become an automatic habit or have become emotionally involved with.

Eventually, you want to be able to form automatic habits which are healthy and positive. However, first you have to add the ingredient that is going to give you the momentum to propel you in a whole new direction. This kind of energy and momentum can only be produced by your emotions.

You might be wondering what your emotions have to do with your eating habits…Let's begin with an example you might already be familiar with:

If you have been following the NBC show "The Biggest Loser," you are probably familiar with Abby. She is a contestant from the eighth season who lost her husband and children in a car accident and gained a whole lot of weight afterwards.

Do you think any of this had to do with her eating habits? Well, yes and no. You see, before she went through the horrifying experience of losing her whole family, she probably had fairly normal eating habits. However, like many people, Abby needed a way to cope with the severe emotional pain she was feeling in her life. Now, obviously you look at someone who lost their entire family and it's not hard to put your finger on the source of the emotional pain.

However, everyone has their own emotional battles to fight and has to find some way to cope with them. For some people it's drugs, for some it's working all the time. Others may choose excessive television watching or video game playing.

For Abby, it was food and the same is true for most obese people. While not everyone's experience is as devastating as Abby's, the level of emotional intensity is all that matters. Some people hate their jobs or are unhappy with their marriage. Others might be stressed about finances, or ironically, about their physical appearance because they are overweight.

No matter what the source of emotional pain or discomfort is food offers a very attractive solution for dealing with it.

How is this possible?

EAT YOUR HEART OUT: FOOD AND YOUR EMOTIONS

If you have ever seen the movie, "Like Water for Chocolate," you'll get an exaggerated glimpse at the relationship between food and the emotions. The movie features a young lady who is such a great cook that people actually become sexually aroused and fall in love while eating her food.

(I know, just bear with me here.)

While this might seem a bit over the top, it's not far from the truth when it comes to how people become emotionally involved with food. You see, your body is wired to help you experience pleasure, and this experience of pleasure is what motivates you to pursue whatever creates that pleasure.

Simple enough, right? Think about five things you would love to experience in the next few days and I bet you a glazed donut that they all involve experiencing some kind of pleasure or they hold the promise of something that leads to the experience of a pleasurable emotion.

And do you know what? I bet at least one of them is a food craving. This craving is not driven by physical hunger it's driven by a desire to experience the pleasurable emotion of eating the food.

You see, pleasure is an emotional need and a very powerful motivating factor. Sometimes this pleasure comes in the form of excitement or happiness, while at other times it comes in the form of security or fulfillment. Sometimes it comes from bonding to others.

Regardless of how we interpret these feelings of pleasure, they all come from the fulfillment of our emotional needs.

Again, these emotional needs are:

- Happiness
- Excitement
- Fulfillment
- Security
- Bonding

These "feelings" are expressions of the emotional component of the human being the ancient Greeks referred to as "the heart." Today we realize that our "heart" is actually the part of us that interprets the emotional vibrations our body is experiencing. We call this state our mood, and this mood is something which can affect your attitude, your behavior, and the results of that behavior. So what is it that creates these moods in your body?

Well, remember how I said your body is wired to help you experience pleasure? The thing I didn't tell you is how your body is wired to accomplish this:

Drugs....sort of.

What I'm talking about here is endorphins. Endorphins are natural "pain relievers" produced by the pituitary gland and by the hypothalamus. They are produced whenever the body experiences something emotionally and physically intense such as pain, orgasm, strenuous exercise, etc.

The interesting thing about endorphins is that the word itself comes from the root words *Endo* and *morphine*, meaning morphine (morph), which is produced by an inner source (endo). As the body experiences a pleasurable emotional state, these natural opiates are released and increase the feelings of pleasure.

Now think about this these are the same little boogers that are released during an orgasm. Your brain interprets it as a state of extreme pleasure and excitement, motivating you to pursue more opportunities to achieve that state.

The same is true with the role endorphins play in the craving for food. The pleasure of eating the food causes the release of a natural pain killer in your body. Considering this, it is not hard to imagine why so many people choose food as a way out of emotional pain.

In fact, you might have experienced this firsthand growing up. Think about it -you'd fall down and skin your knee, and go to mom or dad crying in pain. And what did they give you? A band aid, some Neosporin, and of course, some ice cream.

The natural opiates released by your body in order to fight off the pain of the skinned knee, together with the pleasurable experiences of being comforted by your parent and eating the ice cream create a near orgasmic state of emotional bliss.

I'm not making parents out to be opium dealers. The point is your emotional conditioning has drawn strong connections between eating and the fulfillment of your emotional needs for happiness, excitement, security, fulfillment or bonding to others. Your body reinforces these connections through the release of endorphins, which builds the belief that eating is a quick and easy route out of emotional or physical pain.

Furthermore, research now shows that the consumption of some carbohydrates actually boosts our body's production of the hormone serotonin, which has a calming effect. Interestingly enough, narcotic drugs such as vicodin and ecstasy cause a boost in the body's serotonin production.

The release of these hormones and natural opiates influences the emotional state of your body and sends your body's energy into a positive state of vibration. Are you beginning to understand how people fall in love with food and use it as a way to escape from emotional pain or discomfort?

However, this is not a bad thing.

Thinking of these emotional states as "bad" and trying to suppress the beliefs, desires and cravings associated with them is about as productive as trying to exercise under water. Sure, you could keep it up for a while, but when you come up for air again you are going to gasp all the harder.

In the same way, you can bury and repress food cravings by sheer will. You can force yourself not to overeat. However, sooner or later the rushing tide of these emotions is going to burst out, sending you sprinting to the buffet line, fork in hand.

What is bad is the conditioning and the beliefs associated with these emotional states and this is what needs to change in order for you to achieve your goal weight and stay there for life.

We have already discussed accomplishing this with the use of affirmations and synthetic experiences. However, you might also find that the biggest battle is the one you are fighting when you are not actively engaged in these strategies. That's when you need a strategy you can call upon quickly to redirect your attention to the goal of reaching your normal weight.

Let's start with this question:

WHICH CAME FIRST, THE ANT OR THE PICNIC?

Have you ever wondered how it is that you can go outside to eat and attract every ant within a 50-mile radius? You know how it is they form these well-organized lines and carry away your entire lunch, one morsel at a time.

Persistent little boogers, aren't they?

Well, we're going to beat them at their own game. We're going to put together a plan for getting rid of them all, one at a time, instead of trying to take on the whole mound at once.

In case you think I've gone off the deep end here....let me tell you what ants we're going to get rid of:

Automatic

- Negative
- Thoughts

You know, they just kind of pop into your mind without warning, and little by little they begin to whittle away at your confidence and your ability to remain focused on your goal.

And can you guess where these kinds of thoughts come from? They come from your conditioning. All it takes is one of those emotional triggers to attract the negative thought into the consciousness then suddenly you see your ambition and motivation carried off into the sunset.

Now, getting rid of ANTS is no picnic, but with a little persistence and the right strategies you can exterminate these pests before they get the best of you. You may not be able to stop these automatic negative thoughts from occurring, but you can certainly squash them before they swarm your consciousness.

Let's go back to the original question:

What came first, the ANT or the picnic?

The picnic, of course, is the emotional trigger or experience that attracts the ANT in the first place. The problem is, once these Automatic Negative Thoughts come along, they can ruin what could have been a perfectly normal, emotional experience.

For instance, it's normal to feel overwhelmed, tired or even fat sometimes; we all have those sudden drops in mood. The problem occurs when we allow the moods to control our thought processes and our actions by reinforcing the ANTS, giving them power and life.

In other words, which one came first is not important. What is important is that you find a way to separate the ANT and the emotion that triggered it.

The problem is, most people expend their energy fighting off the ANTS.

For example, if they get ANTS like:

"I can't exercise today it's too hard and I'm tired." "I can't help it; I just want to keep eating."

"I'll always be overweight. I'm not losing weight, so I might as well give up."

They combat these thoughts with statements like:

"No, I can't skip my exercise, because I ate too much. I don't want to stay fat."

"No, I can't keep eating, because I'm overweight."

"No, I don't want to be overweight. I have to lose this weight or I'll feel like a failure."

Now there is a problem with this approach: it simply reinforces the emotional state that brought the original ANT in the first place.

Why? Just read the second set of thoughts again. They're all about negative consequences. They're all about what the person doesn't want. They're all causing the person to imagine that undesirable situation coming about: skipping exercise, eating too much, staying fat, continuing to eat, feeling like a failure.

CHECK ABOVE STATEMENT.

In hypnosis, there is a law called the reverse effect, which states that anytime there is a battle between the willpower and the imagination, the imagination wins. That is because the things we vividly imagine are the things we become most emotionally involved with.

You can will yourself to get rid of ANTS, however, if the thought you are offering up in response is causing you to imagine more negative things....you'll get more negative things.

Just remember the natural laws from last chapter.

So how can you separate ANTS from the emotions that give them power? You starve them. And you do that by neglecting them and choosing to feed other thoughts instead....thoughts about what you really want.

For example, every time you have an ANT, apply the law of polarity and look for the positive side of the situation. Like this:

"I can't exercise today, it's too hard." Becomes:

"If I exercise in spite of being tired, I'll feel so good about having stuck with my goal. This will energize me and encourage me to have a great workout."

And:

"I can't help it; I just want to keep eating." Becomes:

"It's going to feel so great to know that I'm so committed to my goal that I can push my plate away."

And:

"I'll always be overweight. I'm not losing anything and I might as well give up."

Becomes:

"I've hit a wall. How great it will feel to press on and finally break through this barrier what it will do for my self-confidence!"

Just look at the difference between these responses and the previous three. Which ones make you feel more empowered? Which have a better chance at cancelling out the ANTS?

We all have negative moods...some of that is hormonal and can't be helped. However, you CAN help the kinds of thoughts you allow to remain in your mind as a result of these moods and that's what makes all the difference.

Sit down right now and write out five ANTS that occur to you on a regular basis. If you're at a loss, carry a notepad with you in your back pocket and make a note of the ANTS you have as they come.

Next, sit down and write a positive affirmation (remember the SPEAK formula), to combat each one of them. This may take a lot of practice, especially if you have made a habit of negative thinking. However, with a little persistence you'll build a solid line of defense against those ANTS.

Now in case you're someone who has a hard time getting started or being persistent, we have one more law to discuss...

THE SEVENTH AMENDMENT: THE GOYA LAW

If you enjoyed the chapter on the seven spiritual laws, you'll be happy to know that Mother Nature has one more up her sleeve. However, I'm going to warn you that this one has a lot of repeat offenders. The seventh law is the GOYA Law, and it's the absolute, irrefutable secret to getting ALL the other laws to work for you:

- Get
- Off
- Your
- Ass

That's right! It's time to get moving and start focusing on progress and momentum…not perfection.

Perfection (if there is such a thing), is nothing more than the end result of a lot of trial and error which comes as a result of momentum and action. Think about it if you wanted to master archery, what do you think your chances would be of hitting the bull's-eye the first time?

Sounds ridiculous, right?

Of course. So why expect to nail this process down without a LOT of practice, and even….brace yourself my fellow perfectionists…..failures.

You might think the worst thing about never taking action is that you never get what you want. However, in reality the worst part is that you never LEARN what you need to learn in order to be successful.

And how do you learn this? By trial and ERROR.

Yes, I've given you all the guidelines, explanations and evidence, but there's a lot more to come. In the same way, you could sit in a classroom for six weeks and listen to someone lecture about becoming a great archer.

Would this make you a master or even mediocre bowman?

How about ten weeks in the classroom? Twelve weeks? How about six months? One year?

Or how about…

Getting off your ass and putting what you already know into practice?

If you are worried about failure, let me just save you some suspense:

You are going to fail. In fact, I hope you do.

Just don't give up when you do. Instead, examine your results.

Re-examine and adjust your approach. Get back in the game.

Repeat.

Repeat.

Repeat.

Repeat.

Succeed.

Repeat.

This might not sound like the prettiest road, but it's the only way you're going to learn to apply this in your own life. Better yet, it's going to make the reward much more valuable to you when you finally begin to succeed….which won't be long from now, if you just apply the GOYA law.

Now let's get this plan going….

8

Creating Your
NEW IDENTITY

Because people set goals all the time that they never reach; goals they reach only to find that they aren't able to maintain them. Again, this has to do with the role that their identity plays in the attaining and the *retaining* of their goal.

Too often a goal is treated as an arrival point. It's pursued with great discipline and ambition, however, once it is reached, most people abandon the momentum that got them there. The natural response then is to go back to the behaviors that are the most familiar and that are the most consistent with the person's identity.

Remember the frog and the scorpion.

Therefore, the concept of "normal weight" is completely different than the concept of goal weight. Normal weight suggests to your body that this is the appropriate weight for you and that it is the most natural and comfortable weight to maintain.

A goal, on the other hand, suggests something that must be worked for and achieved. It represents an arrival point, instead of a perpetual condition for your body to remain. A goal also suggests to your subconscious mind that you have not yet achieved the weight you're shooting for.

Remember, as you build your synthetic experiences in order to influence your subconscious mind, it's important to see yourself already at the weight you want to be at. Also, the term normal weight suggests to your body that the weight is healthy and....well, normal.

Too often goal weights are set that may not be the healthiest weight for your body. However, a healthy body is really what we want. And that requires you to be at your normal weight, not too thin, not too fat, but just right.

So let's talk about how to set and achieve this normal weight.

TARGET PRACTICE: HOW TO SET THE MARK....AND MAKE IT!

Have you ever heard "Life is a journey, not a destination"? I thought so. When it comes to achieving your normal weight, this is something you want to remember....for good.

You see, a healthy identity is the only thing that can give you a healthy lifestyle; and a healthy lifestyle is the only thing that can give you a healthy body....for life. If you're only interested in having a healthy body for a few weeks, months or perhaps a year, then there are plenty of diet plans out there that can provide you with that temporary patch.

However, if you want results for a *lifetime*, then you have to make a *lifetime* commitment to a healthy lifestyle. This is done through deliberate habit formation, and it is more important than setting goals or following a routine diet plan for 30 or 90 days.

In other words, habit formation is more important than results. Gasp!

Let me explain...

Did you know that the majority of people who win lottery or Powerball jackpots end up spending all the money and are broke within a few years?

Why is this?

It's because they got the results they were after without forming the habits that would naturally attract those results. Therefore, they lacked the habits required to effectively manage those results. You see, people think of habits as a means to achieving or obtaining an end result. However, habits are also required to maintain the results they help us achieve.

Anytime someone takes a shortcut and obtains something without forming the habits required to obtain it, they lose it quickly. That is why it's more important to focus on habits than it is to focus on goals.

If you let the outcome (the goal) go, and instead focus on forming the habits that will naturally get you to that goal, the achievement of the goal is only a matter of time. Furthermore, once it is achieved you can be assured that you have formed the habits required to keep it.

But that's not all…

You must make the deliberate cultivation of positive habits a habit in itself. In other words, you must commit yourself to the continuous practice of cultivating good habits for life. If you neglect to do this, then poor habits will begin to take over as the result of your neglect.

There is no way around this.

It is like caring for a plot of land. You clear the land of weeds and debris first, (getting rid of negative habits), while replacing the empty spaces with seeds to grow good plants (forming positive habits). However, it doesn't end there.

You also have to water and fertilize the ground where you planted the new seeds. You have to continuously remove the weeds that begin to grow in the places where you are trying to grow good plants. Once the new plants break ground, you have to continue to

feed them, prune and water them. In the meantime, you also make sure to remove the weeds as soon as they begin to grow.

This might sound like a lot of work, but it does get much easier as you replace the negative habits with the positive ones. As you continue to work, eventually you will come to a place where cultivating positive habits and fighting off the ANTS is much easier than it was at first.

MUCH easier.

In fact, it can get to be a lot of fun once you get the hang of it. However, you can never abandon the habit of deliberately feeding your positive habits while weeding out the negative ones.

Again, this might sound like a lot of work, but it's MUCH easier than setting goals and trying to accomplish them through sheer discipline, motivation and willpower.

Once you have identified your "normal weight" write it down somewhere, then ask yourself this: what kinds of habits do I need to form in order to achieve and maintain this weight?

The formation of these habits will be used to create a solid plan of action. If you're unsure about how to identify these habits, the following list ought to help get you on the right track:

- Eating habits: how much?
- Eating habits: what kinds of foods?
- Social habits: who do I need to surround myself with?
- Social habits: what kinds of places do I need to spend more time in?
- Social habits: what kinds of places do I need to spend less time in?
- Activity habits: what should I do more of?
- Activity habits: what should I do less of?
- Thought habits: what kinds of thoughts should I entertain?
- Thought habits: what kinds of thoughts should I let go of?

So if positive habit formation is the primary objective, let's talk about how to accomplish it….

THE ROOT OF HABIT FORMATION

Understanding the secret behind effective habit formation begins with understanding the difference between changing your habits and changing your identity.

Henry David Thoreau said, "There are a thousand hacking at the branches of evil to one who is striking at the root."

This quote illustrates the difference between transforming habits and transforming identity. Your habits are the direct result of your identity. In other words, your identity is the root, your habits are the branches, and your results are the fruit.

Imagine this if you wanted to grow apples on a tree, how would you do it?

- Find a lemon tree, pick off all the lemons and glue apples to the branches.
- Dig up the lemon tree and plant an apple tree.

Obviously, the first option would bring you the quickest and easiest result....so why not go with that one? As silly as this may sound, that's where a lot of people put their efforts. However, if you want lasting and fulfilling results in your life, you have to address the root. You have to address the current identity which is in control of your current habits and bringing about your current results.

There is no shortcut, and the sooner you accept this and get to work on the root, the sooner you'll get the lasting results you are after. So let's get started on understanding what a habit actually is. Remember your Four Stages of Learning?

- Unconsciously Incompetent
- Consciously Incompetent
- Consciously Competent
- Unconsciously Competent

A habit is simply a behavior or a set of behaviors from either Stage One or Stage Four. However, the development of a habit can only take place in Stage Two or Three.

Now, we're going to do two things: we're going to work on your new habits and your new identity, simultaneously. As we do this, your habits and self-image will reinforce each other, and set you on an upward spiral toward the development of an entirely new lifestyle.

Many of the exercises we have gone over so far will work wonders for your self-image and habits. However, the following exercises can be used for the deliberate formation of a specific habit and for the deliberate formation of the self-image you choose.

Let's begin with self-image: take the time right now to jump into one of your synthetic experiences. Once you are there, keep your eyes closed and feel yourself living in your new body, at your normal weight.

Once you have a clear image of yourself and you are immersed in the experience, picture a mirror appearing in front of you.

Stop and do this right now and don't open your eyes until you can see yourself clearly in the mirror.

Got it?

Okay, while this is still fresh in your mind, write down a description of yourself using the following questions:

- What kind of clothes do you wear to show off your new body?
- How does it feel to know that you accomplished this on your own?
- How much sexier do you feel?
- What are other people saying about the way you look?
- How does it feel to hear them say these things?
- How much more energy do you have?
- How do you feel about being more energetic and alive?
- How much more do you enjoy physical activities?
- How much more fun can you have because of these things?
- How enjoyable is it to be devoting yourself to good health?
- How is your accomplishment inspiring other people?
- How much more confidence do you have?

Now, you may find that you have to close your eyes and go back to the source in order to answer these questions that's okay. Remember that this is a process and treat it that way. You may also hear a nagging voice in your head that says something like, "*Yeah, but you're still overweight. This is denial. Stop lying to yourself.*"

However, the purpose of this exercise is not to change what is on the outside... not yet. The purpose is to change your self-image and if you focus on changing that FIRST, the outside will eventually catch up. So ignore this voice of doubt, because it's only referring to what is happening on the outside.

Again, the purpose of this exercise is to take care of what is in control of your habits and ultimately your outside results. So it may take your physical image a while to catch up. That's the Law of Rhythm and it's completely natural.

However, if you ignore that long enough to lose yourself in the experience of being at your ideal weight, you'll begin to notice a shift in your thoughts, as well as in your physical vibration. With enough persistence and practice, this state of being will begin to influence your subconscious conditioning and your beliefs about who you really are.

These beliefs will build a self-image and an identity which will inspire you to form the habits to support that self-image. Use this in conjunction with the following exercise on habits, and you'll build a level of momentum that will ensure your success...

The key to habit transformation is being able to stop your old habits dead in their tracks and deliberately replace them with new ones. This will be accomplished through the application of the following process:

- Identify
- Cancel
- Replace
- Reinforce

These four steps are designed to move you from the Unconsciously Incompetent stage to the Unconsciously Competent stage in a clear cut and deliberate manner.

STEP ONE: IDENTIFY THE HABIT

This is where you become consciously aware of the habits that are in the way of achieving your normal weight. Identifying your negative habits requires that you look at all of your current habits (eating, social, activity and thoughts), and ask yourself these two questions:

"Is this a habit that is going to help me achieve my normal weight?" "Is this habit causing the natural laws of the universe, (see Chapter 6) to work for or against me?"

At first you might feel like a one-armed man in the middle of the swamp at night trying to fight off mosquitoes with nothing but a flyswatter. However, in time, you'll begin to recognize patterns in your negative habits and they won't seem so overwhelming.

Most of the time, they'll begin with one of those pesky ANTS, triggered by some kind of emotion. No matter what, once you have identified the habit, move on to Step Two.

STEP TWO: CANCEL THE HABIT

This step is really as simple as it sounds, but it's not always easy. Let's suppose the habit that you're engaged in is going to the soda machine or the snack machine three or four times day. If you're on your way there or standing in front of it, you may end up engaging in a personal battle which will cause people watching to think that you need an exorcism.

This is where the negative anchoring exercises from Chapter Five might come in real handy. On the other hand, if you're going to the refrigerator for a soda or a spoonful of peanut butter, you might want to make it a point to start removing those kinds of temptations until you get habit formation down.

However, most of the time you can simply distract yourself by moving right on to step three...

STEP THREE: REPLACE

Remember how the formation of positive habits is like planting good plants in place of bad ones? Here is the step where you put that principle into practice. Too often, people give up bad habits and then do nothing to replace them with positive habits. This is just like pulling out a bunch of weeds and failing to plant good seeds in their place.

Instead of leaving room for negative habits to re-invade your life, replace them immediately with a positive habit. The best way to accomplish this is to identify what emotional need is being met with the old habit and to find a new and empowering habit which addresses that same need.

Remember the basic emotional needs:

- Happiness
- Excitement
- Fulfillment
- Security
- Bonding

Now look at your old habit and ask yourself, what is it that *I REALLY want to achieve with this habit*? Think about it if you're overeating it's not because your body needs the food. Instead, the overeating is due to a craving for food in order to meet an emotional need.

Too often people who are addicted to things (yes, food addiction is possible) are battling the substance instead of the addiction itself. In other words, they say; "Damn, I need a drink" or "I need a cigarette" or "I really want a piece of cheesecake."

The problem with this, is that it gets their imagination focused on the substance. The Law of Attraction and the law of the reverse effect set in and their imagination of what they don't want overwhelms their willpower.

But that's not all…

They're also not telling themselves the truth about what they really want and perhaps are even unaware of what it is. Therefore, they see no other possibility for addressing their current urge or craving, other than the substance. However, the "need" for any substance that does not fulfill an immediate physical need is always a sign that the need is emotional.

The direct path to overcoming this is to ask yourself which emotional need you are meeting. Sure, it may be hard to identify at first, but if you ask the question persistently enough, the truth WILL emerge. You can also ask yourself this question,

"What am I feeling right now?"

This will almost always lead you back to the emotional need.
For example:

- If you feel sad or hurt, the need is probably happiness
- If you feel bored or trapped, the need is probably excitement
- If you feel hopeless or depressed, the need is probably fulfillment
- If you feel afraid, anxious or uncertain, the need is probably security
- If you feel isolated, lonely or rejected, the need is probably bonding

This line of questioning will take your mind off the disempowering habit and help you to identify a new habit that addresses the emotional need. Here are some suggestions based on the emotional needs.

- **Happiness**: listen to some music that you like, read a book, go for a walk, listen to your favorite comedian or go play with your pet.
- **Excitement**: any of the above or find an activity that challenges, even scares you. (Just be careful!)
- **Fulfillment**: Help someone else or take on a hobby that gives you a greater sense of purpose and meaning in your life. If lack of fulfillment is a persistent problem, you might even want to think about a career change.
- **Security**: Fear is the biggest culprit and it comes from uncertainty. Identify what you are afraid of and put together a plan of action for dealing with it. Direction and action always drive out fear and increase peace and security.
- **Bonding**: Help someone else, call or send an email to a friend, go for a walk, or say hi to at least three people.

Okay, now you have a new and empowering activity. Now, the most important step...

STEP FOUR: RE-ENFORCE

This is the step where most people lose the battle in habit formation, because they don't understand how important it is to reenforce their new habit. In fact, most of us are really quick to scold ourselves when we make a mistake, but we forget to give ourselves that pat on the back when we do something right.

You see, in spite of the fact that your new habit is positive, your emotional conditioning is still going to pull you toward your old habits for a while. Again, this is not a battle that can be won by sheer force of will. Instead, you have to give your new habit a powerful emotional anchor you can associate it with. The anchor will help this new habit become part of your conditioning.

So how can you reinforce your new habits with strong emotional anchors? The same way that we used the negative anchors to discourage your negative habits. As you begin to engage in your new and positive habit, take one of your positive synthetic experiences and associate it with your new habit.

For example, if you have decided to go for a walk instead of getting something from the snack machine, spend that walk imagining yourself in your new body. Really put yourself into the emotional experience and make sure that your subconscious mind will associate that synthetic experience with your new habit.

These four steps will help you to develop a direct route which will take you from practicing Unconsciously Incompetent habits, to cultivating positive habits. Eventually they will become part of your unconscious conditioning.

In case you still have your doubts about the effectiveness of your imagination in achieving the lifestyle of your dreams, let me give you a few examples of people who have already used their imagination in this way.

TO SEE IS TO BELIEVE AND TO BELIEVE IS TO RECEIVE

We have already talked about creating synthetic experiences that engage your creative imagination in the pursuit of your normal weight. However, in spite of how effective the suggestions I have provided, the most effective use of your creative imagination will come from the methods you develop yourself.

This is because people always put more work and effort into the things they help to create. Let me give you a few examples of this:

The Ten Million Dollar Check

You may have heard of the comedic and dramatic actor, Jim Carrey, who was recently cast as Ebenezer Scrooge in Disney's new version of Dicken's "A Christmas Carol." And although he is known internationally as a successful actor, it was not always so.

Carey was not always the actor that he is today, getting paid $10 million or more per movie. Years before anyone knew who he was, he dreamed of being a great actor. One night he sat looking over the city of Hollywood and wrote himself a check in the amount of $10 million dollars. In the memo section of the check he wrote, "for acting services rendered."

Shortly after that night, Carey's father passed away. At his father's memorial service Carey tossed the check into the casket and it was buried out of sight.

However, that very act was enough to create an image in his mind which compelled him to become one of the most successful and prosperous actors alive. At the time of this writing, Jim Carey earns up to $25 million per movie and is one of the most sought after comic actors in show business.

The California Dream Home

Author and entrepreneur, John Assaraf, has a habit of creating vision boards to synthesize experiences about what he wants. (A vision board is a poster-board or cork-board covered with clippings from magazines and other types of pictures which portray a person's goals or aspirations.)

On one occasion John was sitting in his home office in his brandnew house in California. Since he had just moved in, he had boxes of his belongings strewn all over the room. As he was working at his computer, his young son was sitting on top of one of the boxes, kicking it with his heels.

John became distracted by the noise and asked his son to stop. At that point his son asked him, "Dad, what's in this box?"

"Oh, those are my vision boards." John answered. "What's a vision board?"

In order to answer his son's question, John opened up the box and pulled out one of the vision boards. As soon as he saw a picture on one of the vision boards of a house that he wanted, he began to cry.

Why?

Because it was a picture of the actual house that he had just moved into and was now sitting in with his son.

The vision board had been made four years prior to that day.

The Impossible Ford V-8 Motor

Legendary American businessman, Henry Ford, once came to his engineers with a request for them to build an 8-cylinder motor for one of his automobiles.

The initial reaction of his well-educated and highly-experienced engineers was that the creation of such a motor was impossible. Ford's response however, did not acknowledge that the V-8 motor was impossible. Instead it was focused on the specific objective he wanted his engineers to accomplish.

"Produce it anyway," Ford told them.

Six months passed and still nothing from the engineers. When Ford came to check on their progress, they once again reminded him that the creation of the V-8 motor was impossible.

Ford's response?

"Go right ahead. Stay on the job until you have succeeded."

The engineers continued on the job, in spite of the fact that they believed the creation of the V-8 motor to be impossible.

Six more months passed before the engineers discovered the secret that had been eluding them for the past 12 months. Today, the once "impossible" V-8 motor can be found in cars all over the world.

Let me ask you this:

What "impossible" things do you think you might be able to accomplish if you begin to put your imagination to work for you?

How about we find out right now...

NO RETREAT, NO SURRENDER

Bearing in mind that you don't want to push your body past its natural limits, it is time to present yourself with a challenge. Now that you know what you need to know about your subconscious mind, identity, habits, emotional conditioning and the seven irrefutable laws of the universe, it's time to forecast your own destiny.

Let me tell you one other story Napoleon Hill wrote about in his best-selling book, "Think and Grow Rich."

A general once took his army to war to fight against an enemy that greatly outnumbered him. His army landed on the enemies shore and he gave the command to have the ships that had carried them there burned to ashes.

As the ships were going up in smoke, he said to his army:

"You now see that the ships are going up in smoke and that we cannot leave these shores alive unless we win. We now have no choice. We win or we perish!"

They won.

And why did they win? Because they did not allow themselves to even entertain the option of retreat or surrender. This gave them the confidence and the energy to focus all of their attention on achieving the objective.

Too often people underestimate their own ability to get what they want; they fall into the trap of thinking, *"Oh well, if this doesn't work I can always ______."* However, most people are capable of far more than they realize once they realize that there is no way back.

Whatever you need to do today in order to cut out your option for retreat, do it. Maybe you write down your normal weight and the affirmation of the plan you are going to follow and achieve, and sign your own name at the bottom. Maybe you turn around and give this contract to three friends you can count on to hold you accountable until you achieve it. Some people even decide to put money on the line and have someone they trust until they achieve their goal.

Barring some erratic action which might cause you to get in trouble with the law, I recommend that you do whatever you have to, to challenge yourself to achieve your goal.

Think about it the body that you are living in now is the only one you will ever have. You will never be able to trade it in for a new model. When your clock is up, it is up, and there is nothing you can do about it. However, there is plenty you can do starting today that can assure you that the rest of your life will be lived in a body that is healthy and will serve you well the rest of your days.

The time to challenge yourself is right now, and you have almost all of the tools you need to succeed.

Just a couple more things to cover….

9

Living Your NEW IDENTITY

One thing you'll find about a lot of books like this is that they don't always give you a way to fit your new game plan into your everyday life. After all, if you want to make a permanent change, it has to be something that affects your entire lifestyle, right?

That said, I realize that in spite of the great information and strategies I've given you, it is quite possible you will finish this book, and say to yourself: "Wow, that was great!" Then plop it on your shelf next to several other dust-covered, self-help books.

But don't worry, I'm not about to let you get off that easy!

Instead, I am going to give you a few powerful guidelines for making these strategies a permanent part of your lifestyle. Remember, changing your life begins with changing your identity and you are going to need a way to put clothes on that identity and walk it down the street. This means that you are literally rewriting the story of your life with your best self as the hero.

Just remember as we are going through these that your lifestyle is nothing more than an extension of your identity. In fact, you can even think of your identity as the interior element of your lifestyle; it represents the root from which the rest of your lifestyle grows. Trying to change your lifestyle without changing your identity is like trying to run a marathon with a broken leg.

Let's get started with the one element of your exterior lifestyle that has the strongest impact on your personal growth and success…

MISERY LOVES COMPANY....BUT SO DOES SUCCESS!

The great entrepreneur and multi-billionaire, Donald Trump, once said that any person who thinks they know everything and attempts to do it all on their own is doomed for mediocrity. If you want to avoid mediocrity and possibly even failure, it is important to have a strong support system around you.

You might have heard this one: “It's hard to fly like an eagle if you are surrounded by turkeys.” It has been said that you are only as wealthy as your ten closest friends. However, chances are that you are also only as happy, fulfilled and healthy as your ten closest friends.

Now, this might seem like obvious advice, but let's take a closer look...

I realize that I don't need to tell you to get people out of your life (or at least keep them at a distance), when they are clearly discouraging you from pursuing your healthy lifestyle. You already know this is something you must do to succeed at anything.

However, what we need to talk about is getting a positive support system in your life, instead of a negative one.

You see, your “support system” is actually a double-edged sword when you think about it. This is because it is quite possible to have people in your life who are VERY strong supporters of you, but you can still end up being unsuccessful because of their support. This is what I call a “negative support system.”

Let me give you an example...

You start changing your identity and eating habits just as we have been discussing here in this book, but there are still things in your lifestyle which are the same. One of these things is the people that you go to for advice and support when things get tough your friends.

So once you've lost about 20 pounds, you get to the point where you start to get a little too confident, and you start going to the soda machine frequently again. Since you know that this is not going to help you continue to build your healthy lifestyle, you confess to a friend and tell them that you know you shouldn't be doing it.

Now the curious thing about human beings is that sometimes when we make this kind of confession to a close friend, what we are really doing is hoping that they'll tell us, "Oh, it's okay. You've done so well in losing that 20 pounds. A few sodas won't hurt anything." And off we go with alibi in hand, to sabotage our own success.

The same is true for all of us, myself included. Sometimes the support we are really looking for is not the support we need to press on toward our goals. It may be for someone to support our decision to remain in our comfort zone instead of facing the sometimes difficult battle of changing for the better.

This is why it is not always a good idea to go to your friends for support when it comes to pursuing your goals. Certainly your friends want you to be happy and that is the reason they are in your life. However, asking them to hold you accountable can put them in an unfair position and one they would prefer not to be in.

After all, a friend is someone who supports you in the difficult times of life by helping you to be more comfortable and at ease. This is not something that is compatible with challenging you to move out of your comfort zone. Going to a romantic partner or spouse for support can be just as difficult. Again, this is because they are so emotionally involved in your happiness and security.

Surely achieving your ideal weight is going to make you happy, but so is staying in your comfort zone; which is a whole lot easier for anybody to do.

Think about it if your comfort zone had not been making you happy, chances are he would have never gotten stuck there in the first place. So when you go to someone for "support" you have to realize that the kind of support you end up getting won't always be conducive to helping you to achieve your goals.

If the other person thinks that the path of least resistance is supporting you to remain in your comfort zone they may just opt for giving the polite "if it feels good do it" advice.

So what does it mean to build a "positive support system" for pursuing and obtaining a healthy identity lifestyle and body? Well, clearly you know that it means you have to protect your dreams from the people in your life who might discourage you from following you ambitions out of jealousy or some other ulterior motive. The best way to do this is to either write that person out of your life or at least make a commitment to never go to this person for support. In fact, probably a good idea that you don't share anything about your goal with such a person, whether it be good or bad.

After all, if someone is constantly negative, degrading or have the mindset of a victim, they are going to be the first to "support" you in abandoning your goals as soon as things get tough. On the other hand, such a person is probably going to directly or indirectly try to discourage or ridicule you, even when you succeed.

But again, most of us realize these things.

The place where a lot of us slip up is going to our closest friends for support or advice. After all, many of them are in the same place we are and are quick to offer the advice and even rationalizations which have encouraged them to stay there. Keep your friends as your friends and don't put them under the expectation of confronting you with the hard truth if they have to.

Instead, it's time to do what many of us never take the time or opportunity to do in our lives. It's time to connect with someone who will truly inspire you to become your best self and who will set a standard and even hold you accountable when you start to slip...

FINDING YOURSELF A MENTOR

There are two unfortunate things that happen to most of us as we move into adulthood. The first one is that we start to get this crazy idea that there is nothing new to learn and that the educational period of our life is over. The other one is that we divest ourselves of the habit of hero worship. We stop looking for people who will inspire us to be, do and have better lives; people who can serve as positive role models for us.

Since you are reading this book, you obviously haven't fallen prey to the first of these. Good for you. Now it's time to get the second one taken care of...No matter how mature, intelligent, educated or successful you become, it is always important to have a positive mentor in your life.

However, finding a mentor has to be done the right way if you want to get the best results. You see, no one ever achieved greatness out of imitation. A mentor is not someone you try to imitate or become. In fact, any mentor who attempts to get you to do this is probably living out some sort of crazy parent/child fantasy or possibly starting a cult.....just a thought.

Instead, a mentor ought to be someone who inspires you to become your best self and to press on toward your goals. It is someone who encourages you to devote yourself to constant and never ending improvement in all areas of your life.

If you can actually find a mentor you can connect with on a personal basis and spend time with more power to you. However, you might not have the opportunity to even meet your mentor. If this is the case, don't be discouraged.

It is better to aim high and find someone who truly inspires you than to settle for someone just because you can meet them in person. Of course the best case scenario would be to actually have the opportunity to meet with your mentor one-on-one on a weekly basis. However, there is something else you can do that can be just as effective.

Find someone who truly inspires you, someone to whom you can relate. Don't worry about whether you can meet them in person or not. Instead, aim high and make sure it is someone who will set a strong standard of excellence in your consciousness, for you to live up to. This person is your primary mentor.

At the same time, find a person you can actually meet with who will hold you accountable to live up to the standard your primary mentor has set for you. Just make sure that the person you are meeting with has the guts to confront you with respect and compassion when you start to slip. At the same time, it is important that they extend grace to you, and not judge you too harshly when you mess up.

If you are unable to find and connect with such a person, you might want to give serious consideration to hiring a personal achievement coach. Trust me, the investment of time and money will be well worth it in the long run.

However, when it comes to selecting your primary mentor, there are a few basic guidelines I strongly recommend you follow...

First: Look for a Doer, Not Just a Teacher

The world is full of teachers. Doers, however, are in very short supply. In fact, Napoleon Hill stated that it is a basic characteristic of human nature for anyone who has even a smattering of knowledge to offer up their opinion whenever the opportunity presents itself. The problem is that opinions are really just theories and it is not possible for anyone to learn anything from them.

This is probably why Napoleon Hill also said, "Opinions are the cheapest commodities on earth." And why are they so cheap?

Because unless the things someone is teaching are put into practice and used to get tangible results, they have no real value. They are just opinions and opinions have never made any person great.

Instead, look for someone who has convictions. The difference between a mere teacher and a doer is that one of them speaks opinions, while the other lives by convictions. This is the kind of person who can inspire you to become your best self and put your knowledge to work in order to get results.

If the person you choose as a mentor does not have convictions that shape their own identity and lifestyle, your subconscious mind is going to pick up on the duplicity and soak it in until it becomes part of your character as well.

Not cool.

However, if you can find someone who is both a doer and a teacher, then you can be assured that you have found someone who is worth having as your primary mentor. After all, there are some doers whose ability to live by their convictions has become so subconscious that they are unable to clearly explain how they are achieving their success.

Finding someone who has managed to live by their convictions and who understands them well enough to teach them to someone else, is priceless.

A great example of this is Mahatma Gandhi of India. He was a man who lived so strongly by the convictions he taught that he absolutely refused to teach them unless he was living by them.

A young boy who really looked up to Gandhi as a mentor and role model was eating too much sugar and was beginning to become obese, so his mother went to Gandhi for help. She took her son and traveled a great distance on foot so that she could have Gandhi tell her son to stop eating sugar. However, when the woman arrived, Gandhi responded by telling her, "Come back in two weeks."

The mother did not understand, but she trusted his instruction and departed. When two weeks had passed, she once again took her son and traveled the long distance to see Gandhi. Upon their arrival, Gandhi knelt down, looked directly into the child's eyes and said, "Stop eating sugar!"

The mother, a little frustrated, said to Gandhi: "Why didn't you just tell him that two weeks ago?"

"Because two weeks ago," Gandhi replied, "I was eating sugar." Enough said.

Second: Look for Someone Who is Open About Their Weaknesses

It is very important that the person you choose as a mentor does not try to make themselves out to be "superhuman." Let's be honest none of us are invincible. Anyone who comes off that way is certain to end up letting people down sooner or later.

Not only that, but a little flaw in a great person can be a real comfort for the rest of us. It demonstrates to us that greatness is not out of our reach and that you don't have to be superhuman in order to have an extraordinary life. Those who are open about their imperfections are much more secure about who they are and they are worth having as a source of inspiration.

You will even find you are able to relate to a great person's weaknesses and imperfections, which will help you connect with and relate to them better. Even if you never meet someone in person, sharing a common struggle or difficulty often builds a stronger sense of connection with them. This connection will further build your conviction to live up to the expectations your mentor has inspired you to set.

Third: Be Your Own Biggest Fan

I know, I confess I kind of sneaked this one in. You might wonder what being your own biggest fan has to do with finding a mentor who will inspire you…it actually has more to do with the benefit you want from finding a mentor: finding your best self. No matter how much someone inspires you, they are never going to be as involved in your life as you are.

Never.

Your mentor may even let you down sometimes. In fact, you might meet them one day and find that they don't want to give you the time of day and that's okay.

Above all, the role your mentor should play in your life is to inspire you to become the person you were born to be. No matter how much love and adoration you have for your mentor, always make sure that you are the hero of your story.

After all, you are stuck with you for life. Which reminds me…

Finding Your Other Self

If you have ever read Napoleon Hill's work, you'll know that he talks about finding your "other self." No, I'm not talking about developing multiple personality disorder. Napoleon Hill's concept of the other self is about the side of our personality that normally kicks in when our lives start to fall apart.

Think about this was there ever a time in your life when you were faced with a tremendous challenge? Perhaps you had no idea of how to overcome it, but because you absolutely had to meet that challenge, you some how found a way?

How did you do it?

Well, this is where your other self comes in. Remember, your selfimage is the image that is consistent with who you believe you are. Who you truly are is an entirely different story and most of us never get the chance to discover that person. That person is your other self.

For most of us, the other self only comes out when we really hit rock bottom. Since our self-image almost always holds us to a lower standard, the actions of our other self don't have the chance to shine consistently.

The object of the exercises in this book is to help you develop a self-image consistent with your "other self." Sometimes in order for this to happen you have to hit a low point in your life. You may be painfully aware of the repercussions of staying in your comfort zone, but you must be totally excited about the possibilities of breaking out of it.

I can remember one such point in my life.

My father died of liver cancer just as his father before him had. Logically you would think such a chain of events would inspire me to treat a bottle of liquor like a bottle of strychnine. But remember, our behaviors are ultimately not governed by logical thinking processes. They are governed by our emotions.

Whatever hurt, anger, shame or regret I felt as a result of losing my father compelled me to go on a four month drinking binge. Up until that point in my life I had been a social drinker but never allowed the habit to get out of control.

But something was triggered inside me and my body seemed to think that having a drink was the thing to do. I had another, and then another, and then another...

I was still traveling all over the nation, teaching people about staying healthy and overcoming addictions. Meanwhile, I was eager to get to the end of my seminars so I could have another drink.

Of course, there was the usual buffet of rationalizations I used in order to numb my conscience like, "I might be boring if I stop drinking. It's just a few drinks. I'm not hurting anybody. I'm in pain over my father dying." Yada, yada, yada.

But there was still that voice of reason inside that was saying:

"Your father died of liver cancer. His father died of liver cancer. Do you want to be the next in line?" How can you teach this stuff to other people and neglect to follow through in your own life?"

One voice made all the difference and empowered me to overcome the habit. One morning I woke up in my hotel room with my head feeling like an Acme anvil had just been dropped on it and I heard a voice that said:

"This is not who I was meant to be."

The moment I heard the voice was the moment that changed everything. I've never had a problem with alcohol since, nor have I had the desire to touch a drink. A few social drinks here and there, no big deal anymore.

This is because I knew that the undesired behavior was not consistent with who I really was. So how about you?

You might still be angry with yourself for being overweight. You may be sad about it or frustrated. That's simply your body telling you:

"This is not who you were meant to be."

As you continue to apply the strategies in this book, you'll begin to realize more and more that you aren't who you thought you were when you picked it up. You're more than you ever dreamed possible and that's just the beginning.

As your confidence grows, and as you get closer and closer to your goal weight, your beliefs and perceptions about yourself will continue to confirm your new reality. You will become completely transformed, inside and out. Armed with the conscious knowledge of building a healthy self-image, achieving a healthy standard of living, building greater confidence and achieving more profound fulfillment in everything you do.

Bonus Chapter:

IT'S NOT ALL IN YOUR HEAD

Okay, now that we've gotten the difficult part out of the way by changing your self-image and your emotional conditioning, it's time to cover the part that's not in your head. We're going to talk about the role which your metabolism plays in controlling the physical condition of your body.

I could write an entire book about this subject, and most likely will. However, I wanted to activate your brain so that you'll be more aware of what's actually going on inside your physical body as a result of your eating habits and lifestyle. This way you'll be armed with a good knowledge of both the physical aspect of weight loss and the psychological. Think of it like rowing a boat with two oars instead of just one.

You might wonder why I didn't just start out with this chapter...It's because in order for the following information to be useful to you, it must be put into practice. This begins with forming an identity that promotes behaviors which contribute to the cultivation of a healthy lifestyle.

So now that we have that taken care of this information will be MUCH more valuable to you because you'll be able to put it into practice. Let's start out with defining your metabolism and identifying the role that it plays in the condition of your health...

MEET YOUR METABOLISM

The concept of metabolism is so grossly misunderstood by the general public that learning about it is almost like discovering some sacred vault of wisdom which was buried long ago in the sands of an uncharted desert.

You've probably heard people talk about having a "slow" metabolism or a "fast" metabolism...Those who have a "slow" Metabolism claim that their body doesn't burn calories as fast as someone who has a "fast" metabolism. So if you have a "slow" metabolism, you gain weight easier and have a harder time losing it. On the other hand, if you have a "fast" metabolism, you burn calories faster and so you have an easier time remaining thin and fit.

Sorry to do this to you, but it's not quite that simple.

The metabolism is not like this big steam engine that either burns fuel fast or burns it slow. It's more like a complex factory where raw materials (food) are broken down and used either as fuel (energy) or reconstructed into materials which are used to build your body (fat, bone, tissues, muscles, organs etc.).

Taking this analogy, just think about all the variables which contribute to the effective operation of a factory. Speed is not all that matters; you also have to make sure that you have enough control and precision so that materials are broken down and used properly. You have to make sure that when things are built that they are built the right way and that you make the most effective use of the machinery (referring to the assembling of bones and tissues).

You have to make sure that everything is operating at the correct pace and that no resources are being over or under utilized (referring to how your body manages and distributes energy to your cells). You have to make sure that the correct kinds of raw materials are assimilated into the manufacturing process and that the wrong kinds of materials are discarded safely and efficiently (referring to the way that your body determines what nutrients are to be put to immediate use and what nutrients are to be stored).

You also have to have proper procedures in place for managing inventory and for making sure everything is stored properly for later use (referring to fat storage).

If any of these things is out of whack, you can end up with a faulty manufacturing process and therefore a defective product (a metabolism which produces an unhealthy body).

In case you're feeling overwhelmed or intimidated, let's clear up a popular myth about the metabolism. The common assumption about the metabolism is that you just have what you were naturally born with and there's nothing that can be done to change it.

Not true. There is actually a LOT that can be done to change it.

You see, your metabolism is actually determined by something called your endocrine system. This is a fancy word for a group of hormones which determine the way that your metabolism "factory" is run. The cultivation of a healthy metabolism requires proper management of these hormones through your eating habits and your regular activities.

Let's start by having a look at your metabolic workforce...

SPOTLIGHT ON TEAM META

While there are about a dozen hormones which play a major role in your metabolism, we're going to focus on seven of the key players:

1. Thyroid

Thyroid is produced by your thyroid gland which uses iodine from your blood to create the thyroid hormone. This is done in response to a thyroid stimulating hormone which is produced in your pituitary gland. Thyroid determines a whole spectrum of functions which directly contribute to your metabolism, such as heart rate, digestion, rate at which your body burns calories, amount of oxygen used by your cells and even some psychological things like your emotional state.

Having an under active thyroid will cause you to suffer from depleted energy levels and will thus promote weight gain. It is estimated that somewhere around 24 million Americans (whether they know it or not) suffer from some type of thyroid disease. Other studies revealed that nearly 20 million American adults suffer from depression as a result of thyroid disease.

The production of thyroid can be thrown out of whack by consuming foods with excess iodine, having prolonged exposure to stressful conditions, use of certain medications, cigarette smoking, fluoride (found in some of our water supply and in most kinds of toothpaste) and extreme dieting which is based on starvation methods or extreme exclusion of nutrients such as fats or carbohydrates.

When the thyroid is out of whack, someone might experience the frustration of quickly gaining back weight which they have previously managed to lose. Most people who have been "dieting" for the majority of their lives have a thyroid that is out of whack and think that they have a "naturally slow metabolism."

2. Insulin

Insulin is produced by your pancreas; its job is to capture the glucose (sugar) which is in your blood stream after you have consumed foods which are high in carbohydrates or simple sugars. Insulin then takes this glucose to the liver where it is converted into glycogen which is used as energy for your muscles.

This is perfectly normal, until you start to consume too much sugar and your pancreas begins to create excess insulin as a result. This insulin takes as much sugar as possible and converts it into glycogen to be used by your muscles. However, once the muscles have sufficient amount of energy, insulin begins to perform its second task: it begins converting glucose to fatty acids and storing themin fat cells. That's just the tip of the iceberg...

If the body continues to produce insulin in response to increased sugar consumption, the cells of the body eventually build up insulin resistance, which leads to Type 2 Diabetes. High insulin levels can also cause increased sugar craving, obesity, depression, lack of concentration, sleeplessness, bloating and intestinal gas.

3. Testosterone

Most of us think of testosterone as the "male hormone." However, testosterone is also a key player in women's metabolism. In men, testosterone is produced in the testes and adrenals. For women, it is produced in the ovaries and the adrenals. In both men and women, testosterone assists in maintaining a high energy level and in building muscle mass and increasing bone density.

As a person begins to gain excess weight, more of their testosterone is converted into estrogen. This leads to more fat storage which leads to more testosterone being converted into estrogen. This vicious cycle continues causing a person to have difficulty in maintaining healthy weight levels. This is what causes men to develop beer bellies and what is commonly known as "man boobs." Insulin resistance, steroid use, excessive stress and lack of physical activity can also cause depleted testosterone levels.

4. Estrogen

Most of us think of estrogen as these "female hormone." However, estrogen is actually a key player in men's metabolism as well. Estrogen is a steroid hormone which is created out of cholesterol. In the female body, it's produced in the ovaries and fat tissues as well as the adrenals. In men, estrogen is produced in the testes and the adrenals. For women, estrogen keeps insulin and blood pressure levels in check as well as keeping her cholesterol levels healthy. It also helps her to control her mood fluctuations and maintain a youthful energy level.

Unhealthy estrogen and levels come from overconsumption of refined and processed foods. When a woman's estrogen levels begin to deteriorate, she has more trouble controlling her moods and her energy level begins to drop. She will also begin to store fat around her abdominal area rather than her hips and buttocks.

In men, healthy estrogen levels work in harmony with testosterone in order to assist them in building muscle and burning fat. When a man's estrogen levels are not in proper balance with his testosterone levels, he begins to have trouble building muscle and starts to store fat around his hips and pectoral region.

5. Leptin

Leptin is produced in the fat cells and works in conjunction with thyroid and insulin in order to determine how fast your body burns fat and how your body stores fat. The leptin hormone is most active in your brain where it helps control the production of proteins which determine your level of hunger or satiation. Basically, it helps to control the messages in your brain which tell you to either eat or to stop eating.

Excessive body fat causes an overproduction of leptin which leads to leptin resistance in the brain. When this happens, your neural receptors are no longer able to help you determine when to stop eating. This can lead to constant hunger, obesity and depression.

6. Cortisol

Cortisol is produced by the adrenal gland and has a dramatic impact on how your body breaks down proteins, fats and carbohydrates. However, this refers to more than the way that your body takes down the proteins fats and carbohydrates in the food which you consume. It also determines whether your body breaks down stored fat for energy or breaks down bones, skin and even parts of your organs for energy use.

This is what happens when the adrenal gland becomes over stimulated due to excessive stress or anxiety. Excess cortisol also lowers leptin levels and makes it difficult for your body to assess its satiation level and control hunger and cravings.

Now, hopefully you're more than a little bit alarmed by this information. However, considering the things that cause your metabolic workforce to get out of whack, you ought to be encouraged about the amount of control you have over your metabolism.

MANAGING YOUR WORKFORCE

In reading over the details about the six metabolic hormones, you probably noticed that there are some common factors which cause your hormone levels to get out of whack. Because these things are under your control, there are some very practical steps which you can begin to take the day in order to develop a healthy metabolism...

EAT THE RIGHT KINDS OF FOODS

You are what you eat.

Of course, you've probably heard this before your body can only build itself from the things that you eat. But it's important to understand that your body can't always build itself out of the things that you eat. If you eat a paper towel, you're body won't build itself out of that because it does not recognize it as food.

So when it comes to eating the right kinds of foods, it's important to remember that your body does NOT recognize everything that you put into it as food. For example, highly processed foods which contain lots of artificial flavors, colors and preservatives don't "look" the same to your body as natural and organic foods do.

Your body gets confused when you put these kinds of things into it. It doesn't recognize them and cannot absorb the same way that it does natural food. In response to many of these preservatives and chemicals, your body alters its hormone production which creates an imbalance in your metabolism.

However, eating organic foods solves a LOT of the potential problems with your metabolism. It gives your body (an organic system) the right kinds of things to build itself out of and helps your hormones to operate naturally. The result is a more healthy and fit body.

People who eat organic as much as possible rarely (if ever) have problems with their weight.

Now of course, the reason most of us don't eat organic is the "cost" of these kinds of foods. However, there are two reasons why this is not a valid reason to eat processed foods instead of organic. The first is that medical bills are one of the leading causes of personal bankruptcy and the leading cause of financial problems among the elderly. By paying a bit more to eat organic now, you'll save yourself a LOT of money in the long haul.

The second reason is that eating organic foods encourages your body to absorb and USE more of what you eat, which means that you get more nourishment out of organic food than you do out of processed foods. Organic foods also balance your metabolismand help to cut back on cravings and overconsumption. This means you are getting more bang for your buck by eating organic foods.

Just make sure that you know what to look for...

Organic is a relative term for many companies who are trying to cash in on the whole go green trend. Learning to read food labels and recognize natural ingredients will take some time and you won't be perfect at it right away. Think of it as making an investment in your health and in a prolonged life span.

Also, it's important to know that there are specific kinds of foods which you can eat to encourage a healthy metabolism:

- Apples
- Berries
- Barley
- Lentils
- Beans
- Nuts
- Oatmeal
- Leafy Green Vegetables
- Leeks
- Tomatoes
- Green Peas
- Wild Caught Coldwater fish

AVOID EXTREME DIETING

Hundreds of people who have thyroid problems because they have blown out their thyroid through extreme dieting. This includes diets which completely cut out things like fats or carbohydrates or which encourage extremely low caloric intake. Starvation dieting also causes your body to go into a negative nitrogen balance and to begin breaking down its own proteins (organs, muscles, bones etc.) in order to use them as energy. Meanwhile, it holds onto the fat that it has just in case the food shortage gets worse.

Not to mention that a blown out thyroid can cause you to have less energy and initiative to exercise. Exercise is a great way to stimulate healthy hormone production and get your body burning fat naturally, even while you are not working out. If dieting is keeping your body from having the energy and initiative that it needs to workout, the diet becomes counterproductive. This is how people end up having slug slow metabolisms which make it nearly impossible to lose weight and even more difficult to keep from gaining it back.

Stay away from fad diets. Follow the guidelines in this book and achieving, and maintaining, a healthy weight will become second nature.

GET ON A LOW STRESS DIET

When it comes to building a healthy metabolism, cutting excessive stress out of your life will do more for you than cutting out unhealthy fats and sugars combined. If you go back over the above list of hormones again, you'll find that excessive stress is one of the major contributors to hormone problems. If you HATE your job so much that you feel sick on Monday mornings, start working on an exit strategy right away.

Take a pay cut if you have to...if you hate your job there's a very good chance that you are overspending on things like entertainment or eating out in order to make up for the pain of working a job that you hate. Not to mention the impact that I'm sure it's having on your relationships and your happiness. Besides, considering again the long term impact on your health and the rising cost of health care and medical insurance, I doubt that you are getting a better deal by staying at a job you hate just for a bigger paycheck.

Another great way to deal with stress is to exercise. When your body is under stress, it causes excessive production of "fight or flight" hormones. These hormones (like cortisol, norepinephrine and epinephrine) stay in your body and cause you to store fat in unhealthy regions of your body (such as around the belly) and cause all kind of unhealthy food cravings.

Exercise is a great way to give these "fight or flight" hormones a purpose and help you to flush them out of your body. People who exercise also have much higher energy levels so if you think that you don't have the energy to exercise, that's the best reason to start.

Finally, it's important that you identify the sources of emotional pain in your life and deal with them. Most people are in emotional pain when some part of their life does not meet their expectations. This means that these expectations are either unrealistic or are not being met due to lack of action and initiative.

Take one day to yourself and examine your expectations in all areas: health, relationships, finances, and career. Identify which expectations are based on faulty or unrealistic reasoning and let go of them. Then get to work on those which require some kind of action in order to fulfill.

Don't put this off.

Remember the GOYA law and start small. Just start doing *something* to work towards fulfilling the expectations in your life. Even if you don't see results right away, you'll likely feel a LOT better about the fact that you are no longer putting off taking action.

Finally, identify the things in your life that are contributing to your anxiety and clean house. This means the music that you listen to, the movies and televisions programs you watch, even the types of conversations you have. If you find that there are people in your life who are excessively negative or disrespectful to you, start drawing some boundaries right away.

If your spouse or children are included in this list, work on building a better relationship with them by understanding them better. If you've been neglecting them, chances are that they feel misunderstood and undervalued. Make it a point to spend some time making an investment in them so that they feel important. Find out what means something to them and work on fulfilling their expectations for your relationship with them.

While you are at it, take some time to assess your relationships with yourself and work on giving yourself the same consideration that you would want others to give you. You'll be amazed at how this will improve the quality of your other relationships.

CULTIVATE AS NATURAL A LIFESTYLE AS POSSIBLE

The writer, C.S. Lewis, once said that the cause of many of our problems (physical and emotional) is that we are so detached from the natural world. This is well worth remembering as a principle to live by. In fact, I suspect that the reason why so many people fail to understand the natural laws which we discussed earlier is that they don't spend enough time appreciating the natural world.

This does not mean you have to move out into a cabin in the woods, dress in skins, eat only wild berries and chew on ginger root. It simply means that your body is an organic system which requires certain natural elements in order to be as healthy as possible.

First, spend at least 15 minutes outside in the natural sunlight. At least. Spend an hour if you can. If you think that you don't have time, spend your lunch hour outside instead of at your desk or in the break room. Natural sunlight increases Serotonin levels and thus helps you to maintain a healthy energy level and even to fight off depression. If you're curious about this, just read the statistics about depression in places like Alaska where the sun sometimes doesn't shine for months at a time.

Second, get a reasonable amount of sleep every night; eight to nine hours. Any more or less can cause your hormones to get out of whack not to mention that sleep deprivation makes it more difficult for you to deal with stress. Don't fall prey to the myth that you can get by on only five hours a night. You might be able to function on only this much sleep, but you can also run a car without changing its fluids or rotating the tires…at least for a while.

And finally…

GET TO WORK

Remember, the principles in this book are only as effective as you make them. The GOYA law is your friend. Commit yourself to the principles in this book until they become habits, but don't stop there. Keep reaching fora greater level of fulfillment in everything that you do.

A great place to get started is to go to our website and sign up for the 21-Day Diet Program. Go ahead and do this right now at www.markpatrickmedia.com. This is a free email series which will provide you with a step by step game plan to carry you through the first 21 days of your new adventure.

As you practice the principles in this book, you'll feel yourself begin to change from the inside out. The change will be slower at first, but it will pick up momentum as you stick with your commitment. One day, you'll wake up lean, healthy, full of energy and life and feeling great about the way you look, and you'll wonder how you could have ever lived another way.

Till then, continue to dream and to create your own future, first in your imagination and then with your actions. Get to work and always remember that the journey is the reward.

Made in United States
Troutdale, OR
04/15/2026

48530835R00090